Overcoming
Destructive Anger

Overcoming
Destructive
Anger

Strategies
That Work

BERNARD GOLDEN, PhD

JOHNS HOPKINS UNIVERSITY PRESS | BALTIMORE

This book is not meant to substitute for medical care of people with mental health disorders, and treatment should not be based solely on its contents. Instead, treatment must be developed in a dialogue between the individual and his or her physician. Our book has been written to help with that dialogue.

Johns Hopkins University Press
2715 North Charles Street
Baltimore, Maryland 21218
www.press.jhu.edu

Library of Congress Cataloging-in-Publication Data

Names: Golden, Bernard, author.
Title: Overcoming destructive anger : strategies that work / Bernard Golden.
Description: Baltimore : Johns Hopkins University Press, 2016. | Includes
    bibliographical references and index.
Identifiers: LCCN 2015031663| ISBN 9781421419732 (hardback) |
    ISBN 9781421419749 (paperback) | ISBN 9781421419756 (electronic) |
    ISBN 1421419734 (hardback) | ISBN 1421419742 (paperback) | ISBN 1421419750
    (electronic)
Subjects: LCSH: Anger. | Emotional intelligence. | Emotion-focused therapy. |
    BISAC: HEALTH & FITNESS / General. | PSYCHOLOGY / General. | SELF-HELP
    / Anger Management (see also FAMILY & RELATIONSHIPS / Anger). | FAMILY
    & RELATIONSHIPS / Anger (see also SELF-HELP / Anger Management).
Classification: LCC BF575.A5 G65 2016 | DDC 152.4/7--dc23 LC record available at
    http://lccn.loc.gov/2015031663

A catalog record for this book is available from the British Library.

Special discounts are available for bulk purchases of this book. For more information,
please contact Special Sales at specialsales@jh.edu.

Contents

Preface

Anger is a highly charged emotion that's often difficult to understand. Destructive anger—especially if it has led to physical violence—can significantly strain relationships. By selecting this book, you've shown that you are well aware of its impact. Perhaps you blame your temper for a severed relationship with a family member, partner, or friend. Maybe your quickness to anger has caused you to lose a job or has endangered your career. Or, if you have children, your outbursts may have led them to withdraw from you in fear. Whatever the case may be, the greatest test when dealing with anger is to keep it from overwhelming you.

Few people have received instructions on how to manage anger constructively. As such, they often find it challenging. Regardless of how you currently handle your anger, *Overcoming Destructive Anger: Strategies That Work* will teach you the skills to address your challenges and answer your most trying questions. This book offers strategies to overcome anger that

- is overly intense,
- occurs frequently,
- lasts a long time, and
- is difficult to let go.

Overcoming Destructive Anger trains you to recognize and control the triggers that lead to anger. It will help you not only to overcome destructive anger but also to practice healthy anger on a regular basis. You'll learn how to react less to anger, how to identify the unmet needs and desires that contribute to your anger, and how to relate to others so that you more readily meet these needs and desires.

My enduring interest in anger as an adult has been influenced, in part, by my own difficulties with anger as a child. Fortunately, my anger never resulted in serious harm to anyone. However, I did find myself quick to anger on several occasions when it could have caused serious injury and pain to others.

On one occasion, when I was eight years old, I had an altercation with my older brother. At the time, we lived in an apartment on the second floor of a four-story building. We were home alone, and my brother had been teasing me about something. We began to wrestle with each other. He straddled my chest, held my hands to the floor, and pinned me down. I couldn't find the strength to get him off, so I yelled as loud as I could. To be honest, I intended to embarrass him by alerting the neighbors. After wrestling and screaming for a few more minutes, however, I gave up and shouted "Uncle!" and he finally released me.

I may have appeared calm on the outside, but inside, I was furious. As I slowly walked away, I grabbed the heaviest shoe I could find and threw it at my brother's head. With an enviable display of quick reflexes, he ducked. The shoe, however, continued its flight, shattering one of our living room windows and hitting the street below—along with pieces of glass.

I remember immediately feeling ashamed. I had broken the window and destroyed the set of blinds that had covered it, and I feared that the shards of glass might have fallen on someone below. That particular window, you see, was right above the entrance to our building. When I looked out another window, I fully expected to see someone injured as a result of my impulsive anger. Luckily, no one was entering or leaving the building at that moment.

This was just one in a series of events that helped me recognize my difficulty with anger and how quickly I could move from feeling annoyed to experiencing rage. Fortunately, I was also both highly self-conscious and reflective. Perhaps these were early signs of my becoming a therapist.

I eventually vowed to better control my anger, but I usually ended up stifling and trying to ignore it. I had somehow concluded that I shouldn't show or even feel anger. As a result, my anger often escalated until I'd verbally explode and take it out on the next person or situation to cause me additional grief.

Years later, as a young adult, I taught in an elementary school in the South Bronx. During my six years there, I became interested in better understanding the children's anger as well as my own. I obtained my master's degree in psychology, then returned to school full-time for my doctoral degree. For several years afterward, I worked in a psychiatric inpatient setting. I developed workshops to help patients comprehend and control their anger. These early experiences helped me develop the approach I present in this book.

In the 1980s, I began offering workshops on anger management to schools, parents, and businesses, while working in both outpatient and inpatient settings. I've offered monthly classes on anger management since 1994. Additionally, at my private practice, I focus on individual counseling and psychotherapy for the practice of healthy anger.

Overcoming Destructive Anger is for people of all ages. It offers exciting new approaches to anger management that have been developed since my 2003 book, *Healthy Anger: How to Help Children and Teens Manage Their Anger*, appeared. In the vignettes that accompany *Overcoming Destructive Anger*, people learn the causes of their anger and learn to apply the concepts in this book. The vignettes are based on some of my clients, though I've changed certain details to maintain their anonymity. Exercises at the end of each chapter will help reinforce the material, enhance your self-awareness, and cultivate healthy anger.

You can learn specific attitudes and skills to effectively address the full range of your anger, from slight to highly intense. And while you may make significant progress in a relatively short time, creating meaningful change requires commitment and patience. It requires a certain level of *frustration tolerance*: a resilience to endure the discomfort and tension that often arise when learning anything new. *Overcoming Destructive Anger* offers you a way to do this. I thank you for reading this book and wish you success in meeting this challenge.

I am very grateful to the many people who have contributed to the preparation of this book. Like any such venture, it has been supported by the efforts of a team.

Once again, I want to express my deepest gratitude to Nancy Rosenfeld, my friend, agent, and coauthor (with Jan Fawcett) of my first book. She has continued to provide support, feedback, inspiration, and both a gentle and a steady nudge whenever I needed one.

I am extremely grateful to Jacqueline Wehmueller, executive editor at Johns Hopkins University Press, for her consistent encouragement and support throughout. She asked questions and provided feedback that helped me to find direction and clarity in what I wanted to express. I also want to thank the editors who have worked on this project, including Linda Strange, Wendy Lawrence, and Tonya Woodworth. Each provided an invaluable addition toward improving this work. Their feedback has helped me to become a better writer. And I think I have finally come to realize that "less is best." I want to also thank Courtney Bond, production editor, for guiding the transformation of the manuscript into a book.

I am especially grateful to Dr. Patricia Robin, who patiently read the entire manuscript and provided clearly defined and honest feedback to help me further expand on and clarify my thoughts. I am also grateful for the ongoing support of colleagues with whom I share an office.

I have always believed that being a psychotherapist, I must also be a lifelong student. For this reason, I owe special thanks to the many researchers and practitioners whose work has informed my practice and the writing of this book.

Thanks, too, to the many clients with whom I have worked and who have shared of their personal lives.

PART I

Introducing Anger: A Needed But Often Destructive Emotion

CHAPTER 1

Understanding Unhealthy Anger and Healthy Anger

Like all emotions, anger serves a purpose. Just as a baby cries when it needs to be fed or held, a child's or adult's anger typically arises from some form of distress. The baby's cry, a call for assistance, boldly states in a universal language, "I need help!"

Your anger is also a cry for help. You yearn for a release from pain and suffering that you may not fully recognize or even understand. Like the baby's cry, your anger is a fleeting reaction to an immediate sense of unhappiness. You seek compassion, understanding, kindness, and caring. Unlike a baby, however, you can learn to recognize and address your anger and the needs or desires that fuel it. Even better, you can master the skills needed to turn destructive anger into healthy anger.

An Uncomfortable Mind-Body Experience

Anger can occur when you believe that something—whether a person or a situation—is jeopardizing the fulfillment of your most important needs and desires. When you perceive a threat to your physical or mental well-being, your resources, or the people you love, you may defensively focus on whatever has triggered your anger in an attempt to remedy the real or imagined threat.

Your anger consists of a total mind-body experience, one that is tension-filled, based on the interplay of angry feelings, thoughts, and physical reactions within your body. You may think or act impulsively in an effort to

3

release this tension, then later recall "I felt like I was going to explode." Or "I saw red." Or "I just felt like I had to do something." Anger, a distinct and natural emotion, is usually a reaction to and an escape from even more uncomfortable feelings that include:

- shame
- guilt
- anxiety
- frustration
- rejection
- fear
- hurt
- inadequacy
- abandonment
- betrayal

When Should You Be Concerned about Your Anger?

Destructive anger can lead to poor work performance, a stalled career, conflict with others, social isolation, substance abuse, depression, excessive guilt and shame, and even the loss of your freedom. You may find your anger difficult to manage due to its acceleration, intensity, frequency, and/or duration. The following guidelines can help you identify when your anger is a problem:

1. Your anger intensifies rapidly, perhaps "going from zero to sixty" within seconds.
2. Others describe you as a "hothead."
3. You experience mild or intense anger several times a day.
4. You are quick to become aggressive.
5. You maintain a hostile attitude.
6. You often experience anger in your personal relationships, at work, and in daily activities.
7. You have difficulty letting go of anger.

Types of Anger

It's helpful to distinguish among the several terms associated with anger as you begin to confront your own experiences.

Anger is a natural emotion, one that involves an uncomfortable mind-body experience. It motivates us to address our needs, desires, or perceived threats.

Aggression includes behavioral expressions of anger that are intended to harm others. These may be physical or verbal. Aggression can be described as "acting on" and "acting out" our emotional experiences of anger.

Hostility reflects a more chronic and free-floating anger, often accompanied by ill will, mistrust, cynicism, sarcasm, and a general hypervigilance in seeing and subsequently experiencing injustice in one's treatment.

Rage describes the most intense level of anger. Individuals may lose awareness and forget their destructive behaviors during episodes of rage.

Resentment is typically anger that a person clings to, fueling other negative feelings and emotions. When ignored, it can further constrict our view of the world, making us more vulnerable to anger.

Expressions of Anger

People tend to express anger in somewhat predictable patterns. These include aggressive anger, passive-aggressive anger, silent anger, anger denial, and self-directed anger.

Aggressive anger

- is the most serious and problematic;
- is clearly visible;
- may include threats, offensive or hurtful language, physical altercations, or the destruction of property;
- can involve restraining someone against his or her will and is usually loud, intimidating, and fear-provoking;
- often entails some form of personal violation; and
- may require legal intervention.

Passive-aggressive anger

- is subtle;
- usually involves a failure to act, which causes suffering for others or oneself (for example, you may neglect to run an errand for your spouse, or you might arrive unprepared for a meeting at work, affecting your colleagues);
- is intended to hurt, irritate, and undermine others; and
- is often denied when confronted.

Silent anger

- may lead a person to refuse to discuss an issue;
- may present itself as the "silent treatment" and can last for hours, days, weeks, months, or even years; and
- may worsen once others wish to talk about the issue.

Anger denial

- is denied or suppressed anger; and
- is often due to fear of loss of control, rejection, punishment, or the inability to stop one's anger once it surfaces.

Self-directed anger

- is often coupled with anger denial;
- involves a quickness to redirect anger at oneself rather than others;
- can leave a person powerless and pessimistic about satisfying his or her needs and desires;
- can rapidly become overly self-critical and even punitive; and
- often accompanies depression.

Sources of Anger Management Habits

How you manage anger depends on the habits you've developed over time as a result of the interplay of your thoughts, feelings, and bodily reactions. Your quickness to anger, the situations that trigger your anger, and how you respond to anger all reflect patterns from a variety of sources. Like many other aspects of your personality, these habits are based on both nature and nurture—your biological makeup as well as your life experiences—and their combined impact on the neuron pathways in your brain.

Biological Predisposition

Research suggests that a person's unique genetic makeup may contribute to his or her quickness to anger.[1-3] You can easily observe this by waving your hand in front of a baby. Some babies react quickly, frowning or crying or moving their arms and legs. Others seem more passive and show little reaction.

Temperament, a part of your genetic makeup, may contribute to your easygoing, flexible, difficult, feisty, active, slow, or cautious personality.[4,5] These characteristics show up early in life and affect your general excitability. Studies have focused on the major role that hormones, enzymes, and neurotransmitters play in arousing people's anger.[6,7]

Attachment Styles

How consistently caretakers addressed your needs as a child plays a major role in your ability to manage emotions as an adult. Mary D. Salter Ainsworth, a developmental psychologist, performed many early studies on parent-child attachments.[8] These studies involved a child and a caretaker entering a room filled with toys. An observer then studied the child's reaction to that caretaker's presence or absence.

Ainsworth found that some children had a *secure attachment* style. Each of these children demonstrated some tension when separated from his or her mother, but each child also felt comfortable and secure enough upon her return to leave her side to explore the room.

Other children were *insecure-avoidant* in their attachment style. They ignored their mothers whether their mothers left or returned to the room and played with their toys instead. Ainsworth characterized a third group of children as *insecure-ambivalent*. Each child appeared very distressed by his or her mother's absence and could not be soothed when she returned. These children appeared angry or passive. Other researchers later used the term *insecure-disorganized* to describe children who didn't exhibit any of these patterns.[9] These children tended to sometimes approach and sometimes avoid their mothers, possibly recognizing them as both comforting and dangerous.

Ainsworth concluded that children bond securely with caretakers when the caretaker responds to the child's needs appropriately, promptly, and consistently during early childhood.[10] These children develop self-confidence and feel loved and thus lovable and worthy. In contrast, an *insecure* bond occurs when caretakers respond inconsistently, vacillating between appropriate and neglectful. Children of such caretakers experience greater anxiety in their attachments.

Other researchers have explored how these early patterns of attachment shape a person's sense of security and trust in adult relationships.[11] These studies describe adult romantic attachments as (1) *secure*: feeling positive about oneself and one's partner, (2) *preoccupied*: feeling negative about oneself and positive about one's partner, (3) *fearful-avoidant*: feeling negative about oneself and one's partner, and (4) *dismissive-avoidant*: feeling positive about oneself and negative about one's partner.[12] Both anxious and avoidant patterns may lead to more frequent and more intense anger in people suffering from depression.[13] These patterns can greatly influence anger arousal in general, especially in intimate relationships.

Learning

During your formative years, you learned guidelines for managing your anger and emotions from various sources:

- media (television, radio, books, magazines, movies, music, video games, and the Internet)
- parents
- siblings
- peers
- clergy
- teachers, relatives, and other adults

You received these messages both directly and indirectly. The direct messages provided specific expectations and rules for managing anger. For example, your parents were direct if they told you not to raise your voice when angry. They may have reprimanded you for fighting with your peers or siblings. Or perhaps they reminded you to "hit back when someone strikes you" or to discuss your anger in words rather than showing physical or verbal aggression.

In contrast, you may have observed others' behavior—in indirect messages—to learn how to govern your own behavior. For example, if your father yelled at your mother, he modeled both how to handle anger and how men and women should relate to one another. Whether your mother withdrew, cried, or talked back further modeled how to handle anger. How your siblings managed their anger also helped you develop your own methods of coping with anger.

You may have learned about anger from how others expressed anger toward you. Being yelled at or hit—if either happened to you—may have appeared to directly communicate anger. However, such behaviors

represent indirect messages because feelings aren't directly discussed. And yet, this kind of anger can have very powerful and lasting effects. I'm not suggesting that one scolding or slight hit on the bottom will scar a person for life. Such discipline does, however, convey the message that physical aggression leads to power. It also offers children few opportunities to better understand their feelings.

I've worked with many clients who minimized how such actions affected them. They often downplayed their suffering to protect themselves from feeling angry and helpless about such circumstances.

Whether your caretakers listened to and validated your feelings during moments of emotional suffering also taught you how to handle anger. For example, suppose your father disapproved when you showed pain. Or worse yet, he shamed you for it. This experience may influence how comfortable you are with your feelings today.

If you're a man, your caretakers might have encouraged you to follow the "Boy Code," which suggests that real men never show anxiety, anger, or self-doubt.[14] Ironically, adhering to this code often leads to destructive anger as a way to escape from shameful feelings (see chapter 9).

If you have a sister who was indifferent to your suffering, this might have indirectly warned you to avoid relying on others to help alleviate your pain. Unfortunately, this can leave you feeling depressed and isolated, contributing to anger.

Many of these direct and indirect messages are inconsistent. Some people believe that all anger is destructive and should be avoided. Others think that anger is okay as long as we don't show it. And some suggest that we should just "let it all hang out" and do what feels good, regardless of how it affects others. Clearly, many of us have learned conflicting guidelines about how to cope with our anger.

Brain Science

In recent years, neuroscientists have used functional magnetic resonance imaging, or fMRI (a variation of magnetic resonance imaging that measures blood flow and blood oxygen level to form a functional image of the brain), to explore how our brains contribute to our anger arousal.[15,16] Some, such as Allan Schore, focus on the mother-infant relationship and how it affects the brain. Schore has redefined attachment theory as *regulation theory*.[17] He believes that development of the brain system that regulates

emotions depends on our mother's interactions with us in early childhood. Mothers can aid brain growth by being sensitive to a child's excitability and helping him or her manage its intensity. Early interactions substantially affect our reaction to threats and negative emotions in general.

Studies further emphasize the role of the *amygdala*, an almond-shaped mass located deep within the brain. The amygdala, along with the *hypothalamus* and the *periaqueductal gray*, forms a neural system often called the "threat system." Part of the "primal" or "old brain," this system controls arousal as well as emotions such as fear, anger, and pleasure.

Your amygdala sends impulses to the hypothalamus to activate the sympathetic nervous system, which is involved in the fight-or-flight response. This part of the brain holds your emotional memories. In contrast, your *prefrontal cortex*—often considered the "new brain"—is responsible for high-level reasoning. It processes information to determine whether action is needed and controls how impulsively you react to threats. As shown throughout this book, these systems significantly influence your feelings of anger and your anger arousal. Every exercise in this book helps you actively engage your new brain—your reasoning—when confronted with a real or imagined threat.

Keep in mind that your attitude and everything you've learned about anger are embedded in your brain's neural pathways.[18] When you repeatedly get angry in the same manner, the neurons in these pathways create strong connections, forming your habits. But neuroscientists say that people can reeducate their brains. Cultivating new ways of thinking and responding can lead nerve cells to form new connections to other neurons, creating and strengthening new patterns in your brain and new habits. This concept of *neuroplasticity* is fundamental to this book.[19] You can change how you manage anger regardless of how you've done so in the past.

What Does Anger Look Like?

By looking at several examples, we'll see how anger can distract people from feeling threatened. We'll also see the negative emotions that accompany anger and what can make a person respond with anger.

Twenty-nine-year-old Jerry, a computer program consultant, described his reasons for attending my anger management class:

Well, it's happened enough times. Now my boss told me I have to take this class. I know I get angry a lot at work. I yell at my coworkers. And I'm sarcastic with my clients. Sometimes I actually ridicule them. Oh, yeah, I apologize afterward. But by then, it's too late. This time I'm really afraid of losing my job.

Marielle, the mother of two young children, reported feeling severely ashamed over her tendency to yell at and demean her three-year-old. She detailed her experience as follows:

I'm so afraid I'll hit her. I'm afraid I'll be just like my mother! I swore I'd never be like her, but I just can't seem to stop myself. Shelly is so stubborn. And she won't listen to me. She is so stubborn! That's when I lose it. At least I know I need help.

Brent, thirty-one years old, had a long history of hostility affecting his personal life and had put off seeking help for several years. He shared the following:

My anger has gotten in the way of almost every relationship I've had. Only once have I ended a relationship. The other three times my girlfriends couldn't take it anymore, and they left me. I never hit them, but I often came close. I'd break things instead. Several times I've thrown a lamp or a glass against the floor or wall. This time, I really love my girlfriend and don't want to lose her. I hope it's not too late.

Jerry worried about losing his job due to his anger issues. He was often quick to feel threatened and experienced intense emotions of anxiety and inadequacy when clients asked questions. He directed his anger outward to avoid these uncomfortable feelings. Gaining greater self-awareness enabled him to pinpoint the anguish that had provoked his anger in the first place.

Marielle experienced intense guilt over her anger. She felt threatened by a loss of control over herself and her daughter. By adopting the practices in this book, Marielle came to recognize the deep suffering—the sense of inadequacy and worthlessness—that fueled her anger when her child challenged her. She realized that her daughter's behavior aroused feelings of powerlessness, which Marielle had experienced with her own mother. As you will discover throughout this book, pain from recent events as well as from the distant past—a past that a person has not fully mourned—often leads to intense anger in the "now."

Some people can harbor a hostile attitude for their entire life. It can appear in every arena of one's relationships. In Brent's case, his fear of loss pushed him to seek help. He knew that his early experiences made it difficult for him to trust others. His father died when Brent was six years old. By the time Brent was twelve, his mother had remarried and divorced twice. His quickness to feel threatened and his tendency to become overbearing in relationships were attempts to avoid feeling hurt and abandoned again. Domination and anger became his main strategies to exert control over his life, especially with the people he cherished the most.

Jerry, Marielle, and Brent became more self-aware as they explored and came to better understand their intense anger. None of them spontaneously changed their habits, but they took a significant step toward responding constructively to anger. They learned how past hurts might have sensitized them to the experience of threat and anger. And finally, they learned to be more assertive when interacting with others so they could more effectively satisfy their core wants and needs. They acquired new ways to react less to their anger. These new habits are best described as aspects of healthy anger.

Healthy Anger

You may at first question the notion that anger can be healthy. So, before going any further, I want to define healthy anger:

1. Healthy anger means observing and experiencing your anger without being overwhelmed by it and reacting to it.

2. Healthy anger means recognizing your anger as a signal to explore the feelings, thoughts, and bodily sensations that precede it.

3. Healthy anger means viewing anger as a signal to look inward to identify your core desires, needs, and values.

4. Healthy anger calls for developing self-compassion, which includes skills to enhance your sense of safety and connection.

5. Healthy anger includes developing strategies to let go of anger, which may include forgiving others and yourself.

6. Healthy anger encompasses practices that don't cause suffering for others or for yourself.

7. Healthy anger means learning how to communicate assertively with others.

8. Healthy anger enhances your resilience and overall well-being.

9. Healthy anger requires you to develop compassion for others.

The Pathway to Healthy Anger

The pathway to healthy anger presented in this book uses skills from three broad areas of understanding and practice: *mindfulness and mindfulness meditation, self-compassion,* and *self-awareness.* Here, I briefly describe each of these areas of study.

Mindfulness and Mindfulness Meditation

Mindfulness and mindfulness meditation (further explored in chapter 3 and throughout the book) can help you examine your own experiences without reacting to them or becoming overwhelmed. Specifically, these practices teach you that your thoughts, feelings, and physical reactions are only temporary rather than a fixed part of who you are. This gives you the increased freedom to choose how to react to them.

Self-Compassion

The pathway to healthy anger offered in this book is based on practices and research associated with *compassion-focused theory* and *compassion-focused therapy.*[20] This work, in turn, is based on cognitive behavioral therapy combined with evolutionary, social, and developmental theories; Buddhist psychology; and neuroscience. It finds that your brain has evolved to emphasize three motivational forces. One force helps you seek and maintain safety and alerts you to potential threats. A second force—ideally, experienced in early childhood and in your most loving relationships—centers on your need for warmth and a connection to others. The third force moves you to strive for life fulfillment, enabling you to focus on your goals and how to achieve them.

Compassion should also be practiced to arouse calmness and to feel safe. Mindfulness supports self-compassion and self-compassion supports mindfulness. Together, these practices allow you to stop overreacting to anger and to experience healthy anger through choice instead.

Self-Awareness

Mindfulness and mindfulness meditation and self-compassion help increase self-awareness. They foster and strengthen your intention to practice healthy anger. However, healthy anger depends not only on being mindful of your experiences in the moment but also on becoming aware of and understanding your thoughts, feelings, and bodily sensations and how they interact. Self-awareness can also help you achieve future goals by aiding in your ability to make a commitment. This is essential to meeting your most basic needs for life fulfillment and motivation.

* * *

As you embark on this path, you may encounter a number of internal experiences that arouse discomfort and compete with and inhibit your journey. These potential blocks to healthy anger are detailed in the next chapter.

For Further Reflection

1. How do you currently manage your anger?
2. In what situations do you experience anger?
3. How does your anger negatively affect you and others?
4. As a child, what direct messages regarding anger did you receive from your father, your mother, and others?
5. As a child, what indirect messages regarding anger did you receive from your father, your mother, and others?
6. What messages from the media—including television, music, video games, and the Internet—do you believe influenced your views and behavior regarding anger?
7. What have you experienced in adolescence or as an adult that may have had a strong impact on how you manage anger?

CHAPTER 2

What Are the Challenges to Cultivating Healthy Anger?

Take a moment to observe what you're experiencing right now. Are you feeling enthusiastic and motivated to continue reading? Or cynical? Are you relaxed or apprehensive? Is your body calm or tense?

I ask these questions so that you'll become more aware of your inner experiences. Such awareness is key to practicing healthy anger. It's also especially important for recognizing those thoughts and feelings that discourage you from practicing healthy anger—in spite of your strong desire for change.

The strategies you've used to manage anger over the years have served a purpose. They've developed in response to your feeling threatened and have become, in effect, an "emotional armor." So, although you may want to learn new strategies, you may have difficulty letting go of these older, seemingly protective habits.

This chapter identifies habits that may keep you from mastering the skills needed to practice healthy anger. You could be reacting to some of these habits when you misplace or stop reading this book, decide to do something more fun, or find a variety of other reasons for not committing to change.

Thinking *You Should Change Your Habits Is Not the Same as* Feeling *You Should Change Your Habits*

Your response to your own anger is rooted in years of practice. For this reason, you may not *feel* like you want to change even though you *know* it's in your best interest to change. The phrase *child logic* best explains this.

Child logic occurs when emotions dominate your reasoning. This type of less-developed, childlike thinking can keep you from noticing the finer details of each encounter or experience. As a result, you may feel threatened even when no real threat exists. A child bitten by a dog, for example, may fear all dogs because he or she can't understand that not all dogs are dangerous.

Child logic has little to do with your intelligence or age and is so ingrained that you're unaware of its impact. It plays a major role in what you expect of others and yourself. It can also lead you to quickly jump to conclusions when confronted with a triggering event. Simply stated, the emotional brain dominates the logical brain, leaving you hypersensitive to perceiving threats and vulnerable to impulsive thoughts and behaviors.

Your child logic intends to protect you from harm. So, although you may firmly believe in practicing self-compassion and healthy anger, your child logic can undermine this goal.

You Are Familiar with Who You Believe You Are

We're all creatures of habit. We often behave in the ways that are most familiar to us. Because we're familiar with who we think we are, we may view our personalities as fixed and unalterable. You may cling rigidly to this sense of self, fearing you'll lose your identity if you abandon old habits. I've often heard clients say, "I won't be the same person if I give up my anger." This is partially true. Your personality is fluid rather than fixed. While you may remain the same in many ways over a lifespan, each new life experience redefines you to some degree.

Practicing the skills in this book will lead you to change. Cultivating healthy anger will have a positive impact on your relationships with others, with the world in general, and with yourself.

Anger Works

Anger can be extremely rewarding in the short term. It can distract you from pain and threatening feelings. You may use anger to provoke fear and anxiety in others. Such anger makes others feel threatened, allowing you to gain control. But regularly directing anger at someone is likely to make him or her even less supportive. Ultimately, that person will withdraw completely—leaving you feeling even more isolated.

Tension Often Accompanies Learning New Skills

People often feel uncomfortable when learning new skills. This is understandable. Consider the skills you've already developed—whether playing an instrument, mastering a computer program, or speaking comfortably in front of an audience. The most tension usually occurs when first learning a new skill—due to feelings of self-doubt, impatience, or awkwardness. Conquering new skills requires *frustration tolerance*. We must manage these temporary, uncomfortable feelings in order to accomplish our goals. We must believe in ourselves and realize that mistakes are a part of learning.

You may see this as a powerful threat to your grandiose child logic that says "new learning should be easy" or "I should know such skills without having to learn them." Worse yet, you may believe you should be perfect. These anxiety-provoking thoughts often lead us to abandon our efforts to learn new skills.

You Enjoy the Physical Rush That Accompanies Anger

When you get angry, your body releases *cortisol*, a hormone that helps you respond to stress. You may experience a positive physical "rush" that overrides any self-doubt and makes you feel alive and energized. Fueled by child logic, however, this rush diminishes your capacity to use good judgment.

It's hard to stay aware of your internal experience when you're feeling threatened. Practicing healthy anger for long-term gratification requires assertiveness, which is deeply satisfying and empowering.

You Hold on to Anger to Avoid Taking Responsibility

It's not always easy to make decisions. And anger can distract you from having to take responsibility for your decisions. It's often much easier to blame others for your suffering.

I've worked with hundreds of people who have held on to anger toward parents, siblings, employers, partners, exes, or others they believed to be responsible for their misery. Some felt thwarted in pursuing their dreams and clung to resentment for decades. They often blamed others for decisions made long after those people were out of their lives.

You may know the consequences of holding on to anger but deliberately choose to avoid responsibility, like Jake, a participant in one of my classes:

> I know I'm chasing my fiancée away with my anger. But, you know, I don't want to have to take responsibility. I don't want to have to control my anger. I was the oldest child in a family with three other siblings. My father died when I was eight, and I feel like I've had to take responsibility my whole life.

Jake wanted to hold on to his hurt and anger because he believed that life was unfair to him. He wasn't yet ready to let his anger go.

Your Dependency Needs Undermine Your Taking Responsibility

Learning to practice healthy anger requires your commitment, even when you don't feel fully up to the task. It's especially challenging if you refuse to mourn the loss of "what could have been" and keep looking outside yourself for compassion. Or, you may be yearning for someone to fill an "emotional hole" left by unfulfilled needs. Perhaps, without being aware of it, you hope someone else will take care of you and rescue you from your anguish. To satisfy this need, you may focus too much on your partner, your job, your children, or even your religion. Your tendency to rely on others for care-taking may cause you to overlook two very important concepts: Others may love you, but it's ultimately up to you to define the structure and meaning of your life and to take the steps to live it. And others may treat you with compassion and love, but it's your responsibility to be open to accepting them and to feel compassion toward yourself.

Self-Reflection May Be Uncomfortable

Throughout this book, I'll encourage you to self-reflect, which can sometimes feel very uncomfortable, for a variety of reasons. The more harshly you judge your feelings, the more difficulty you may have in acknowledging them. Additionally, you may experience painful emotions that have long remained dormant, masked by anger or other distractions.

To a great extent, self-reflection requires solitude. It requires alone time and peace and quiet so that we can focus our attention inward. Our culture's pressure to be social and to win others' approval all too often overpowers our desire for solitude. It's in our nature to want to feel like we truly belong. And yet, both solitude and reflection are essential for allowing us to solidly connect with our beliefs and values. Although the ability to have a loving relationship with another person is often seen as the true measure of mental health, the capacity for solitude is equally important—and is too often overlooked.[1]

Unfortunately, you may view self-reflection as a sign of vanity or weakness. As a child, you may have felt responsible for the happiness of a parent, sibling, or other relative. You may have become so preoccupied with caring for others that you've lost sight of your own needs and desires.

Perhaps you became critical of self-reflection through messages that devalued it. My clients often share comments reflecting this, such as being told "You're thinking too much," "You're overthinking it," or "Just keep busy if you're in a bad mood."

Other Activities May Be More Rewarding in the Short Term

Cultivating healthy anger requires effort and commitment. Many activities are certainly more immediately gratifying than self-reflection. In fact, people commonly seek fun, short-term pastimes rather than activities that provide deeper and more lasting gratification. Giving priority to your need for amusement may compete with your practice of healthy anger—just as it can cause you to put off other goals. You need to be able to look at the big picture and judge the long-term benefits of healthy anger. This practice supports frustration tolerance, which is essential to self-discipline.

Your Anger Undermines Your Effort

Your anger may disrupt your commitment to this program. You may harbor resentment at having to do it. You may resent others who don't share your difficulties with anger. You may also dislike the time and effort required to be kinder toward yourself.

It's natural to compare yourself with others at times. Certainly, some people will seem more resilient to life's challenges than you are, while others will find these issues harder to work through. Such comparisons only keep you from identifying and working on what you truly need to move past your quickness to anger.

People hold on to resentment when they haven't fully accepted where they are at the moment. They haven't fully mourned their expectations about "where" or "how" they should be. As such, any comparison with others can undermine the self-acceptance, mourning, and commitment that are necessary for change.

How You Can Expand Your Awareness to Challenges

The following guidelines will raise your awareness of the challenges facing you. They can help you to be mindful of your thoughts, feelings, and bodily sensations as you cultivate new skills for healthy anger.

1. Review this chapter and identify those challenges that may have the strongest impact on your commitment to practicing healthy anger.

2. Identify five outcomes that you hope to achieve by practicing healthy anger.

3. Seek out others who are genuinely available to support you. Unfortunately, there are often more "discouragers" than "encouragers" when it comes to making changes in one's life. Seek out the encouragers.

4. Refer back to this chapter frequently to determine which, if any, of these challenges are affecting you at any given time.

5. Practice the exercises described in later chapters that address how to respond to and move past the influence of these challenges.

Gradually, as you move forward, you'll increasingly *feel* right about your desire to change and not just *think* you should embrace change.

* * *

Your ability to be aware of these challenges requires being attentive to their arousal as you read this book and practice the exercises. Mindfulness and mindfulness meditation, as described in the following chapter, can help you foster such attention.

For Further Reflection

1. When you were growing up, what messages did you receive regarding self-reflection, self-exploration, and self-curiosity?

2. When you were growing up, what messages did you receive regarding the use of anger to control others?

3. Are you holding on to anger toward someone in your past to avoid the anxiety of taking action in your life? What are you keeping yourself from doing?

4. How might you be alert to those challenges that can undermine your commitment to healthy anger?

5. While others may contribute to your anger arousal, you are ultimately responsible for how angry you become and how you manage it. At this very moment, think about your reaction to this statement. How does it make you feel when I tell you that you are responsible for what you do with your anger?

CHAPTER 3

How Mindfulness and Mindfulness Meditation Can Help

Anger, a powerful and challenging emotion, can hold your attention hostage. This makes perfect sense for your "primal" brain. When you feel threatened, you may automatically focus only on feeling safe again. This will hamper your ability to engage your "rational" brain to understand your anger and respond to it constructively.

To practice healthy anger, you need to realize when your attention is narrowing—before the anger overwhelms you. Both mindfulness and mindfulness meditation can help you achieve such awareness.

Eastern religions have included the practice of mindfulness and mindfulness meditation for almost two thousand years. In recent decades, Western mental health researchers have studied the effect of these practices on both emotional and physical well-being. They've found that mindfulness and mindfulness meditation effectively treat anxiety, depression, chronic pain, and addiction and improve the quality of life.[1]

Practicing mindfulness while working toward healthy anger will allow you to more easily

- observe and experience your thoughts, feelings, and sensations as transient events that pass by like clouds in the sky;
- view your thoughts, feelings, and sensations as products of your mind that don't truly define you or your situation;
- identify those needs and desires that reflect what you value most in life;

- recognize the emotions, thoughts, and bodily sensations that may predispose you to anger;
- recognize opportunities to intervene and affect your anger early in its development and progression;
- identify unrealistic expectations, which foster unnecessary suffering and anger; and
- lessen the quickness and intensity of your emotional reactions.[2]

Mindfulness

Mindfulness requires you to expand your curiosity and observe your thoughts, feelings, and bodily sensations—as well as observe what's occurring around you. Mindfulness calls for being self-compassionate, nonjudgmental, gentle with yourself, and aware of your humanity. Jon Kabat-Zinn defines mindfulness as "moment to moment, nonjudgmental awareness, cultivated by paying attention . . . as non-reactively, as non-judgmentally, and as openheartedly as possible."[3]

Think about what you're experiencing at this very moment. What do you hear? People, a television or radio, birds, or the siren of an ambulance racing down the road? Do you smell anything? Is the air around you dry or humid, still or moving? Look around you. Notice the details of what you see. Can you identify colors, textures, and forms? By answering these questions, you've engaged the senses that inform you about your environment.

Now, direct your attention inward to how your body feels against the floor, chair, or couch you're sitting on. Are you comfortable or tense? Is your stomach grumbling? Are you experiencing any other physical sensations?

Now notice your thoughts. Are you considering what to eat when you finish reading? Are you aware of any thoughts or emotions related to the challenges discussed in chapter 2, such as frustration or irritation at having to change how you manage your anger? Don't dwell too much on the content of your thoughts.

And finally, observe your feelings. Are you anxious, calm, or annoyed?

Mindfulness—with respect to developing healthy anger—requires you to observe and "sense" rather than "analyze" your inner experiences, just as you might notice the vivid blueness of the sky, the rich taste of your morning coffee, or the beep of the alarm clock that begins your day.

Psychiatrist Daniel Siegel suggests that we possess a sixth sense in our ability to observe sensations in our body and a seventh sense in our ability to observe our thoughts, feelings, memories, hopes, and dreams.[4] Being mindful helps ground us in the now rather than in the past or future.

Try the following exercise to see just how vivid your observations can be when you fully immerse yourself in the experience.[5]

EXERCISE

Eating Mindfully

Place a raisin (or any dried fruit) in your hand. Move it around between your fingers and palms. Imagine you're a child who has never seen this before.

Hold the raisin up and give it your full attention. Look at its color variations. Note the light and shadows in its folds and its unique features.

Move the raisin in your hand, touching it with your fingers and palm. Close your eyes if it helps you focus better.

Hold the raisin to your nose and deeply inhale its aroma. Note any subtle changes in your mouth or stomach.

Gently place the raisin on your tongue. Notice your hand moving and your mouth opening as you do this. Without chewing, move the raisin around with your tongue and explore its shape and texture.

Place the raisin between your teeth. Notice the movement of your mouth and tongue while doing this. Then slowly bite into the raisin. Notice the impact it has on your tongue. Note its texture and taste as you chew. Try to be conscious of your intention to swallow before actually swallowing.

Notice any taste remaining in your mouth and sense any movement as the raisin travels to your stomach.

Observe your reactions to this exercise and any thoughts or feelings you experience after completing it.

Mindfulness can help you realize that angry thoughts and urges are fleeting experiences you can choose to ignore. Mindfulness can help you experience anger and its accompanying feelings without becoming overwhelmed. It's all about being fully aware, even when an experience is unpleasant or uncomfortable.

The ability to tell yourself "This is the thought I'm experiencing now" or "This is the feeling I'm experiencing at this moment" helps you realize that *you* are the observer and in control. This awareness allows you to ponder the choices available when responding to your anger—without overreacting.

Mindfulness may not fully remove the sting associated with your experience, but it helps you to sit with it and let it be. As we'll explore later, mindfulness can show you that rigidly holding on to unrealistic expectations can contribute powerfully to anger. For example, mindfulness can help you see that "others should behave as I think they should" is just a thought. You can simply observe it or fully believe it to be true.

Mindfulness Meditation

Various forms of mindfulness meditation exist in Buddhist philosophy and in Western adaptations. Vipassana is one of the widely used approaches to help cultivate mindfulness and self-compassion. *Vipassana* means "looking into something with clarity and precision, seeing each component as distinct."[6]

Ram Dass describes mindfulness practice as seeing "your thoughts go by as if they were autumn leaves floating down a stream. The leaves drift by, being moved this way and that by the eddying water . . . the leaves, the thoughts float by, but keep your attention on the water itself."[7] Mindfulness meditation lets us more easily observe ourselves without judgment. The moment we think about an experience, we're no longer observing it. With practice, we can increase our capacity to sit with and witness whatever we're experiencing in any given moment. This is a cornerstone of the practice of self-compassion.

Mindfulness Breathing

In the long-standing tradition of meditation, observing our breathing has been used as a starting point for such focus. Breath sustains life and constantly reminds us that we're alive. It provides nourishment that doesn't require our attention. As such, we don't seek to control or avoid it.

We cannot store our breaths for the future. Any breath we take occurs and then passes. Our breathing anchors us in the now—the present moment. Engaging in mindfulness breathing can counter our tendency to become too attached to our thoughts or feelings.

Various mindfulness breathing techniques are possible. The following approach is based on those in *The Mindful Way through Depression* and *Mindfulness: An Eight-Week Plan for Finding Peace in a Frantic World.*[8,9]

EXERCISE

Mindfulness Breathing

Prepare yourself. Wearing loose clothing, find a place where you won't be disturbed. Sit on the floor or in a chair. *Floor:* If you prefer the floor, sit on a cushion that's high enough to let you cross your legs in front of you on the floor. This reduces strain on your legs or pelvis. Keeping your spine straight, drop your shoulders so that you're relaxed. Then place your lower arms, with hands facing up, over your thighs or in your lap. *Chair:* Alternatively, you can sit in a straight-backed chair. Rest both feet fully on the floor. Sit upright while keeping your spine straight. Place your hands on your thighs so that your shoulders can relax. Close your eyes if that feels comfortable, or lower your gaze.

Be aware of your body. Spend a few moments focusing on the sensations in your feet—including your toes, soles, and heels—as they touch the floor. Then note any sensations in your body where it contacts the floor or chair. Spend a few moments with these sensations.

Focus on your breathing. Breathe slightly faster or slower until you reach a comfortable rhythm. Notice the breath entering your nose and moving down into your lungs, feeling the movement of your diaphragm. Feel your chest rise and fall as the air moves up and out through your nose. If helpful, place your hand on your abdomen to feel its movement as you inhale and exhale. Or, note the air moving through your nostrils. Focus on your abdomen or your nostrils for thirty seconds as you sense your breathing slow and your body relax. Continue to notice the sensations of breathing.

Observe your wandering mind. Eventually, your mind will wander, and your thoughts may scatter in different directions. This is natural. It's how the mind works and doesn't reflect any weakness or failure. You once again become aware of your experience at the moment you recognize your mind has wandered. Note where your mind has been and then focus your attention on the rhythmic pattern of your breathing as your breath goes in and out.

Note your thoughts. If you think you're doing this incorrectly or poorly, just note these thoughts and gently bring your attention back to the sensations associated with your breathing. Continue for five to ten minutes.

What were your reactions during this exercise? The only goal is to observe your experience, note it, and then ease your attention once again back to your breathing. Some highly competitive individuals strive fervently to empty their minds. Others report feeling energized or relaxed. And some report becoming very tired and sleepy. Many are simply surprised or even annoyed with how active their minds are.

Your mind may have drifted to thoughts of daily chores, important issues, or even self-criticism. Perhaps you tensed as your focus turned inward, as if you were violating some deeply entrenched code you had sworn to obey. You may have experienced negative feelings such as sadness and anxiety. Just note them for further exploration at a later time. While mindfulness is a way for you to sit with your thoughts and feelings, it's not about ignoring the important issues in your life.

This practice emphasizes our breathing. Buddhist monk and author Thich Nhat Hanh states: "Each time we find ourselves dispersed and find it difficult to gain control of ourselves by different means, the method of watching the breath should always be used."[10]

Most of us prefer pleasant thoughts, emotions, and bodily sensations over uncomfortable or painful ones. And yet, expecting no discomfort only contributes to our misery. Mindfulness is about recognizing that our attempts to avoid negative experiences cause much of our emotional turmoil. Mindfulness means fully accepting our internal experiences and realizing that much in life is beyond our control.

With regard to healthy anger, mindfulness entails acknowledging our emotions and how they influence our moods, attitudes, and actions from moment to moment. Being mindful allows us to better identify the forces that shape how we view ourselves, others, and the world around us.

By sitting with your observations and noticing your reactions, you become more sensitive to your inner world. Repeating this process allows you to treat internal experiences in this way even when you're not meditating. You view your thoughts and feelings as things to observe rather than as permanently defining your state of being.

Strengthening Your Commitment to Mindfulness Meditation

Practicing mindfulness meditation means embracing new habits. The following guidelines identify key elements to consider as you move forward:

1. Pick a specific time of day to practice.
2. Select a specific place to practice.
3. Identify the benefits to you at the beginning of each practice.[11]
4. Begin by practicing for five to ten minutes.
5. Commit to at least one week.
6. Use visual cues—whether in the form of a poster, photo, note, or other object—that remind you to practice.
7. When your attention shifts to challenging thoughts and feelings, acknowledge them and gently refocus on your breathing.
8. When you find yourself judging or overthinking, note this and redirect your attention to your breathing.
9. Keep in mind that it's unrealistic to expect all practice experiences to be similar or different.
10. "Being in the now" can arouse anxiety, for a number of reasons.
11. Recognize the tendency to experience *monkey mind*, a mind that jumps restlessly from one thought to another.[12]
12. Remember that regardless of your mood, meditation expands your capacity to be present with your experience without being overwhelmed.

In addition, remember that thinking you're "not good" at mindfulness meditation, that your mind won't stop, that it's a waste of time, or that you spend too much time on one specific thought is temporary. Note the thought and focus on your breathing. (See the resource section at the end of the book for downloads and websites that offer guided meditations.)

Practicing Principles of Mindfulness Informally

Your day is filled with opportunities to practice mindfulness principles even when you're not meditating. On waking in the morning, you may choose to be mindful of the various sensations of stirring from sleep and rising to face the day. You may notice the gradual shift in muscle tension in your neck as you raise your head from the pillow or in your legs as you move to stand. Similarly, you can note your thoughts and feelings as you go from deep sleep to full wakefulness.

Take time to practice mindfulness as you shower. Pay attention to how the water feels as it hits your skin and cascades to your feet. Notice the water's temperature.

Walking easily lends itself to being mindful. Focus on how the muscles in your legs and feet feel as you take steps and make contact with the ground. You can practice mindfulness meditation by pacing back and forth over the same area while keeping a natural rhythm. Find a place where you can walk safely while attending to your breathing.

Taking your *mind-body pulse* (assessing your feelings, thoughts, and physical sensations) a few times daily is another way to cultivate mindfulness. This might simply entail engaging in mindfulness breathing. As you take your mind-body pulse, you may find it helpful to close your eyes to avoid distractions. Such routines make it easier to remember to be mindful.

Focusing on your breathing is a powerful way to stay in an observing mode rather than a thinking or doing mode. Doing this just a few minutes a day can better acquaint you with the different modes. It also will help you to make mindfulness a natural part of your routine. I use public transportation and often take a few moments to attend to my breathing as a way to relax and feel more centered.

Informal mindfulness practice can also involve noticing the details of what's around you. You can practice mindfulness while grooming your dog, by feeling his coat and watching how the comb's teeth move through his fur. Or, try practicing mindfulness while brushing your own hair. Pay attention to how the bristles on the brush feel as they move across your scalp.

Household tasks such as washing dishes provide yet another opportunity for informal mindfulness. Observe the soap suds on the dish and the effect of wiping a sponge across it, or inhale the soap's clean fragrance. Then shift your attention and observe your thoughts, feelings, or bodily sensations while performing this chore.

I often pause to be mindful of the sounds and sights of my surroundings while walking in a park or running an errand. At such moments, I can choose what I wish to be mindful of and switch my attention to different sensory "channels." I may be thinking about where I'm going or my plans for the day. Tuning in to the sounds around me—birds, conversations, traffic, or even the wind—takes me out of my head and redirects me to my current life. Listening to music also offers an opportunity to practice mindfulness. When your mind wanders, gently return your attention to the music.

Waiting is a perfect time to practice mindfulness breathing. You can do this while in line at the supermarket, sitting in traffic, or waiting for a friend to arrive for dinner. While talking with a friend, try being attentive to her words, tone of voice, or facial expressions. You may find yourself mindfully attending to your own thoughts, feelings, and sensations in reaction to what your friend has shared. These are all forms of applying the principles of mindfulness to your everyday life.

As I write this chapter, it's a beautiful early June day. A few clouds are widely scattered across the bright blue sky, and the temperature is perfect. I'm experiencing a strong urge to go outside to enjoy the day. Perhaps this is because I live in Chicago, and we've just endured one of the most brutal winters in years.

I could pretend this urge doesn't exist. I could try to talk myself out of it and remind myself that I'll have other such days in the coming weeks. I could tell myself that it's just another wintery day, and all those people I see wearing summer clothing are simply fooling themselves.

Each approach falls short of accepting my urge as a natural and passing experience that I don't have to react to. I don't attempt to avoid this urge or block it out. I don't force myself to dream about nice days in the future to replace the urge. I gently redirect my attention to writing. By doing so, I remain open to any ideas that might unfold, as well as the pleasures or frustrations of the writing process.

Mindfulness and Healthy Anger

Mindfulness practice can help you merely observe, instead of act, when your immediate impulse is to respond to events that trigger anger. You'll learn to choose a different pathway when it comes to the content and quality of your expectations. Similarly, being mindful of your thoughts after a triggering event can help you take steps to reduce your anger. And being mindful of the emotions preceding anger offers increased self-awareness, which can help you connect with others and yourself. Most significantly, you'll become increasingly able to recognize and satisfy your needs and desires based on what you most deeply value.

Unfortunately, many people tend to practice mindfulness only when they're actually meditating. I saw a poignant example of this once while standing in a rather long line at my bank. It was a late Friday afternoon. Of the eight windows available, only two had tellers stationed behind them; the other six windows were closed.

A woman entered the bank, stood behind me, and abruptly shouted, "Why aren't more windows open? Is this how you run your bank? Get more tellers to the windows! I have other things to do!" Almost in unison, everyone turned to see who had screamed so impatiently.

Barely a minute had passed when another woman entered the bank. The woman behind me immediately greeted her with "Hi, Judy. How are you? I missed you at meditation class." For whatever reason, the woman behind me had failed to use her mindfulness meditation skills to deal with her anger. If she had, perhaps she would have been assertive rather than aggressive in voicing her concerns.

Some people practice mindfulness meditation as a relaxation exercise that has little to do with the rest of their lives. In fact, some people meditate to avoid getting in touch with their feelings and thoughts. Mindfulness isn't a substitute for looking inward to better understand how we habitually feel or think. Rather, it can help us to do so with greater openness and acceptance.

* * *

Mindfulness practice calls for self-compassion. The next chapter will help you understand such compassion, how it relates to mindfulness, and how it supports the practice of healthy anger.

For Further Reflection

1. View "The Monkey Business Illusion" by Daniel Simons on YouTube for a delightful example of the challenges of multitasking.[13] It shows how limited our attention really is—which can affect our mindfulness practice.

2. When practicing mindfulness meditation, you might experience some doubts about it (for examples, refer to the challenges in chapter 2). You may think, for example, that the practice has deep religious overtones—which it doesn't. Or you may believe it's only for those who have time to meditate while on a beach by the ocean or that you must attend a weekend retreat before you can begin or be really "good" at it. Most importantly, be mindful of the discomfort you'll feel when you experience monkey mind. Remind yourself that the more you practice mindfulness, the more you'll simply observe this experience without it affecting you.

3. What thoughts and feelings did you experience while reading this chapter? Did you experience any of the hurdles mentioned in chapter 2, such as the discomfort of learning new skills, the wish that change could be easier, or the challenges of self-reflection?

CHAPTER 4

The Role of Self-Compassion

To a great extent, your capacity for healthy anger rests on your ability to summon and accept self-compassion. To deal with the hurt associated with anger and to let go of anger, you must develop self-compassion.

Recent neuroscience research shows that certain practices in self-compassion can rapidly and dramatically heighten your sense of safety and calm.[1] Feeling calm in your mind and body frees you to explore the thoughts, feelings, and bodily sensations that are a part of anger arousal. These practices broaden your ability to be mindful of your internal experiences as they unfold into anger.

Mindfulness and Self-Compassion

Paul Gilbert, the founder of compassion-focused therapy, defines the term *compassion* as follows: "Compassion can involve a range of feelings, thoughts, and behaviors such as those aimed to nurture, look after, protect, rescue, teach, guide, mentor, soothe and offer feelings of acceptance and belonging—in order to benefit the target of one's caring."[2]

Self-compassion implies that you can be compassionate toward yourself. It is a term frequently associated with Buddhism and has only recently received formal study in the West. As psychologist Christopher Germer says, "Self-compassion is a form of acceptance. Whereas acceptance usually refers to what's happening *to you*—accepting a feeling or a thought—self-compassion is acceptance of the *person* to whom it's happening. It's acceptance of ourselves while we're in pain."[3]

Just as compassion depends on empathy toward others, self-compassion means being sensitive to your own suffering.[4] It requires you to separate the "experiencing" part of you from the part of you that's "observing" what you're experiencing. Your observant side can then "step back" and experience empathy with your distressed side. Self-compassion offers you the emotional resilience to work through your experience even when it's painful.

The Components of Self-Compassion

When first introduced to the term *self-compassion*, many people immediately conclude that it simply means being able to love oneself. But self-compassion means more: it means developing attitudes and practices that foster a more complete and deeply felt love and respect for oneself. Kristin Neff, psychologist and author of *Self-Compassion*,[5] highlights the components of self-compassion:

- kindness with oneself
- recognizing and honoring one's humanity
- mindfulness[6]

Kindness with Oneself

Practicing kindness with yourself is a fundamental component of self-compassion. When practicing self-compassion, you see yourself from an objective, parental, nurturing, and wise perspective. While the Golden Rule encourages you to treat *others* as you want them to treat *you*, self-compassion involves treating *yourself* as you want others to treat you. You're mindful of how you treat yourself and choose to be compassionate in that relationship.

Kindness to self involves kindness to all of yourself. When it comes to anger, self-compassion requires you to deal with yourself in a kind, gentle, and more empathetic fashion. This can help you access your feelings, thoughts, and bodily sensations, slowing anger arousal. Self-compassion also enables you to identify your core needs and desires and what gives you meaning. With self-compassion, you show kindness not only to positive experiences but also to those that cause discomfort or even pain.

As you'll discover in chapter 9, the body is the source of our emotions. A key component of being kind to yourself involves listening to your body to distinguish your feelings and emotions. The body, rather than the mind, senses safety and threat first.

Kindness to yourself doesn't mean satisfying every desire. Self-compassion entails being mindful of what's in your long-term best interest. It contrasts sharply with self-indulgence. It doesn't support telling yourself, "I'll be kind to myself. I'll eat another piece of cake, even though it's in my best interest to diet," or "I'll treat myself kindly. I'll buy that car, even though it will be hard for me financially." Rather, self-compassion involves kindness to yourself that's mindful of what is healthy or most constructive. It moves you to seek resources that can help you achieve long-term goals.

Self-compassion embodies neither self-pity nor self-indulgence but rather a healthy affirmation of ourselves. It entails *positive self-regard*: a belief that we deserve to experience less pain. True self-compassion doesn't encourage self-absorption or passively accept suffering. Instead, it motivates us to move past our anguish by experiencing it rather than ignoring it.

Kindness involves being mindful of our needs and desires. The kindness of self-compassion is especially relevant to anger. It allows you to recognize anger as a signal that you suffer underlying pain that must be addressed. Being kind to yourself means knowing your needs and desires and being able to distinguish between them. This is a starting point for alleviating anguish. It's the groundwork for identifying constructive ways to satisfy your needs and desires.

Recognizing and Honoring One's Humanity

Practicing self-compassion helps you to honor your humanity. Self-compassion is about being mindful of the fact that you're human—imperfect and flawed. It keeps you striving to improve yourself while recognizing that you can only do your best.

For a moment, envision yourself as the object of a Google Maps search, seen from a satellite miles above Earth. You zero in on an image. You see your continent and then your country. You recognize your neighborhood and then, there you are—just one of millions of people who share this planet. I'm not trying to make you feel small or insignificant. Rather, I'm reminding you to keep things in perspective. You're a part of humanity regardless of your state of mind at any given moment and no matter how alone you feel. You face many of the same struggles as the rest of us. You're human when you make mistakes, fail to live up to your standards or those of others, hide from shame—and yes, even when you've shown destructive anger. Remember that others have felt the same because they're human too.

All too often, people fail to acknowledge their humanity, which leaves them feeling isolated and weak—and as a result, they are vulnerable to anger. Some people seek perfection in a futile attempt to gain acceptance. They fail to realize that feeling like a part of humanity isn't attained by achievement. Nor is it defined by wealth or power. Rather, feeling that you're a part of humanity stems from the relationship you have with yourself.

The most meaningful act of self-compassion involves working to ease our own pain while realizing that suffering is a natural part of life. Doing it successfully requires us to be fully conscious of our humanity, our strengths, and our weaknesses.

Being human means we feel. When we compare ourselves with living creatures that aren't human, we often ask, "Can they feel? And if so, what do they feel?" We fully recognize that our broad range of emotions makes us human. We may proudly view this as a distinguishing strength that maintains our superiority to other creatures. And yet, it's ironic that we so often wish to take flight from these very same feelings.

Self-compassion involves fully embracing the feelings that make us human. It's the antidote to experiencing shame about what we feel. Any attempt to ignore our feelings robs us of a piece of our humanity and our ability to fully know ourselves. So the good news is that we feel. The disturbing news is that we sometimes have disturbing feelings.

Being human means we all suffer. Regardless of what we wish for or what we do, we all experience loss, disappointment, and other misfortunes. We're all vulnerable to illness—no matter how much we might believe otherwise—in spite of miraculous advancements in medicine and in spite of fully embracing self-compassion. And, ultimately, we all die.

All too often in recent years, good parenting has been equated with protecting children from frustration and suffering. As shown by one of my clients, this sometimes leads to the unrealistic expectation that we shouldn't have to suffer.

Forty-three-year-old Vanessa entered my office exhibiting sadness in every aspect of her being: she walked slowly, eyes downcast and filled with tears, and spoke quietly. Within minutes she transformed into a woman full of rage. She loudly and angrily informed me that she had been diagnosed with cancer. She ranted about having no family history of the disease, always watching her diet, exercising, and doing everything right. "How could I have this horrible disease?" she asked.

Certainly, she was tremendously upset and understandably angry. She was fearful and anxious about her future. It soon became clear that she found it terribly unfair that she should have cancer. She believed that she was special, that only others got sick, and that she didn't deserve such a fate. She was right only in her last assumption. By thinking of herself as special or immune from misery, she failed to recognize her humanity. We become even more vulnerable to hurt when we forget or deny that being human involves suffering.

Mindfulness

Self-compassion requires us to be open and sensitive to our thoughts and feelings without suppressing or denying them. Mindfulness entails being nonjudgmental about what we're thinking and feeling, without pressure to change.

Nonjudgment as a component of mindfulness involves accepting that we live our lives as best we can with the awareness we have at any given moment. It's easy to look back to the past—be it ten minutes or ten years ago—and see what we might have done differently. Hindsight is a good thing if it keeps us mindful the next time we face a similar situation. It's the opposite of self-compassion, though, if we repeatedly berate ourselves with "could haves," "would haves," and "should haves."

Judgment originally developed to protect us. It served as an alarm system to address perceived threats. However, such judgment can betray our true self. It distracts us from what we find meaningful and leads us to feel alienated from ourselves and others. Furthermore, judging our emotions only arouses our anger more quickly, whether we direct it toward others or ourselves. This is why nonjudgment is critical not only to self-compassion but also to healthy anger.

Recognizing and Evoking One's Wisdom

Wisdom is another major component of self-compassion. *Positive psychology*—a branch of psychology that emphasizes our strengths—defines *wisdom* as "knowledge and experience" and "its deliberate use to improve well being."[7] Researchers of positive psychology, such as Martin Seligman and Christopher Peterson, emphasize that a wise person has self-knowledge built on self-reflection. As Tibetan Buddhist teacher Khandro Rinpoche says, "The human heart is basically very compassionate, but without wisdom, compassion will not work. Wisdom is the openness that lets us see what is essential and most effective."[8]

Possessing wisdom means being aware of what you know and of what you don't know. Wisdom provides structure and guidance to help you decide what's in your long-term best interest. And wisdom can keep you from impulsively acting on thoughts or feelings that affect you only in the short term.

Research on wisdom, using neuroimaging techniques, reveals an interaction between the new brain and the old brain.[9] In effect, wisdom activates both the rational mind and the emotional mind, but the rational mind wins out in a conflict between the two.

Evoking wisdom channels anger in a healthy manner. Your wisdom is built on a reservoir of past experiences that you can draw on to decide what's truly in your best interest. Such wisdom is always growing. Studying and practicing the approaches suggested in this book is one way for you to expand your wisdom. And, as explained in the next chapter, drawing on imagined experiences is another way to access your wisdom.

Self-Compassion and Healing

As psychologist Kristin Neff poignantly points out, "To give ourselves compassion, we first have to recognize that we are suffering. We can't heal what we can't feel."[10]

Practicing mindfulness, self-compassion, and self-awareness is essential for recognizing pain. Together, they help us to observe without over-identifying with what we feel or think. As described by Neff and others who study self-compassion, *overidentification* occurs when our emotions overwhelm us and cloud our perception of what's really occurring.[11]

Tyler, who was referred to one of my classes following an incident at work, offers an example of this. He shared the following with the group:

I'd just met with my supervisor for my annual evaluation. He told me that my overall rating was "average." He said that my rating would have been better if I'd met my deadlines more consistently. He also felt that I needed to be more assertive. I couldn't believe him! I wasn't expecting that. I was furious. I worked hard this past year and put in a lot of extra hours. And I don't deserve to be treated this way. I told him that. I explained my views for about fifteen minutes, but I got nowhere. He wouldn't change my ratings. I finally got so mad that I cussed at him, and then I told him I was going to the human resources director.

Tyler was caught by a variety of feelings. He certainly felt disappointed and frustrated. Most importantly, he felt he was treated unfairly. Anger overwhelmed him, and he wasn't sufficiently self-compassionate to sit with those feelings. Instead, he immediately lashed out. These feelings only strengthened when the next day, his supervisor suspended Tyler for two days and told him that he needed to attend an anger management class.

We can overidentify with depression, anxiety, shame, guilt, and other negative emotions. And when we do, our thinking narrows, and we're unable to entertain different thoughts that could help us satisfy our needs or desires. As a result, we may focus exclusively on our anger.

Avoiding pain requires effort. It can distract us from fully connecting with ourselves. All too often, we take flight from our feelings instead of stopping to note and care for the pain we're enduring. We may *know* that life involves pain, but we *feel* we shouldn't have to endure it. We may *know* that life isn't fair but expect fairness anyway. These perspectives prevent us from accepting our experiences. They also force us to magnify and hold on to our pain and further increase our suffering.

Dwayne, a young father, sought help after becoming increasingly enraged with his five-year-old son, Egan. Dwayne's anger had increased since the birth of his second child, who was now three. He recalled his interactions with his wife and his older child:

Egan just doesn't listen to me. And my wife lets him get away with a lot. We just don't agree on how we should discipline the kids. She's so much more lenient than I am. I repeatedly tell him to pick up his toys, but he just doesn't listen. My wife doesn't even get upset. And lately, she'll tell him a couple of times and he listens.

Through the practices described in this book, Dwayne realized that his anger toward Egan had many sources. He felt powerless when his child refused to listen. At those moments, he also believed that his wife failed to treat him with the respect he deserved. Since the birth of their children, Dwayne and his wife had become increasingly distant. He felt neglected in many ways. And as much as he loved his children, he harbored some resentment toward them as well.

Additionally, part of Dwayne's anger toward his son stemmed from his attitude toward his own father. Dwayne was raised to fear his father. "When he told me what to do, I jumped. I always listened to him. I was scared of what would happen if I didn't. And Egan doesn't seem to have any fear of me."

Dwayne had minimized and denied the hurt and anger he'd experienced at the hands of his own father. He became convinced that such parenting was both necessary and effective. Consequently, he was unaware of the need to be caring and compassionate toward his own child.

Practicing self-compassion helped Dwayne recognize a variety of feelings that had lain dormant for many years. He subsequently identified ways to address his hurt and anger issues.

* * *

We've explored the components of self-compassion, its relationship with mindfulness, and its contribution to the practice of healthy anger. All the remaining chapters provide practices that integrate mindfulness, self-compassion, and skills for self-awareness.

For Further Reflection

1. Being uncomfortable with compassion or self-compassion may inhibit your practice of healthy anger. It's essential that you're aware of what you truly feel and believe regarding compassion and self-compassion. I encourage you to try the following exercise.

EXERCISE

Compassion

Look at the word *compassion*. Be aware of any thoughts, feelings, or mental images that arise as you do so. For example, you may recall times when you received, gave, or observed compassion. Or perhaps you find your mind is blank. Become aware of any bodily sensations you may feel just thinking about compassion. Be especially attentive to any tendency to view compassion negatively. Do you find yourself becoming uncomfortable or wanting to avoid the experience? Do you find yourself emotionally and physically cringing in annoyance or even disgust?

Such discomfort may come from child logic, which informs you that you're weak and vulnerable to need or want compassion. Most importantly, it may stem from child logic that's overly influenced by self-disgust and believes you don't deserve loving kindness. You may also find compassion repulsive if you fear revisiting a painful time in your life when you needed compassion but didn't receive it. All of these experiences deserve and require compassion if you're to move past them.

What direct and indirect messages (see chapter 1) have you received regarding suffering?

What direct and indirect messages (see chapter 1) have you received regarding compassion?

Identify an experience in which you showed self-compassion. What were you thinking during this experience? How did you feel as a result of it?

2. Anger may be understood as an attempt at self-compassion. Unfortunately, when it's destructive, it can best be described as self-compassion gone awry. Identify ways in which this description of anger is accurate.

PART II

Using Mindfulness and Self-Compassion to Overcome Destructive Anger

CHAPTER 5

Cultivating Self-Compassion

Cultivating self-compassion requires you to be acutely sensitive to your relationship with yourself. It involves mindfully embracing attitudes and behaviors that reflect self-compassion. The practices here will help you to choose self-compassion as part of your pathway to healthy anger.

What Kind of Parent Are You to Yourself?

To be self-compassionate, you must be alert to your attitudes toward yourself.

1. How do you view yourself when you make mistakes or fail to live up to your expectations?

2. What do you tell yourself about your suffering and the feelings that foster or accompany it? What do you tell yourself about your feelings in general?

3. How do you judge physical pain? How do you care for your body?

4. Are you a good friend to yourself?

5. How hard do you push yourself to achieve? What content and tone of voice do you use to motivate yourself?

So, what kind of parent have you been to yourself throughout your life? This question may seem odd at first. But you began to parent yourself very early on. Even though others may have parented you during your childhood, you often also parented yourself. You began to develop an internal voice—a "voice of authority"—at a very young age. This voice established what you should expect of others, the world in general, and, most importantly, yourself.

As a young child, you listened to this voice very closely, sometimes without being aware of it. In many ways, it's been the voice guiding your daily decisions and behaviors, and it has

- defined who you were, who you are, and who you wish to become;

- helped shape your attitudes toward yourself when you did or didn't live up to your own expectations; and

- had an impact on the relationship you have with yourself.

So, what has been the overall quality of your voice? Is it the voice of compassion or of tough love? If you've been compassionate, your relationship with yourself reflects the qualities discussed in chapter 4. If you've been practicing tough love, you may have learned to numb yourself to the pain of living. Like many whose real parents used tough love, you may show distrust in your relationships. You may set highly unrealistic goals for yourself and compare your achievements to others' rather than experiencing satisfaction with your own accomplishments.

Tough love leads to feelings of inadequacy. As a result, you may experience most relationships as competitive struggles. And quite often, tough love leads to a need to control, a defensive and cautious way to avoid feeling inferior. The voice of tough love inside you may even cause you to turn sympathy with yourself into self-pity.

Becoming Compassionate to Your Experience of Anger

Practicing self-compassion helps you sit with your feelings in the same way a parent might sit beside and reassure an upset child. It requires you to show compassion to every aspect of your internal experience of anger—your needs and desires, expectations, assumptions, negative feelings, bodily reactions, and mental images. Comprehensive self-compassion means striving to be validating, empathetic, and sympathetic with yourself and with every element of your experience.

Validation

Compassionate parents validate their children's feelings by listening to them without trying to fix, deny, or minimize those feelings. As adults, this enables us to fully accept our feelings without judgment rather than avoid them.

Empathy, Sympathy, and Compassion

Empathy with others involves feeling the feelings of another person. Being empathetic with yourself requires you to recognize and identify your own feelings.

Sympathy, in contrast, is caring about how others feel and wishing them a rewarding and joyful life. Being self-compassionate means embracing this attitude with regard to yourself.

Empathy and sympathy help you to witness, sit with, and experience your pain. Being aware of and empathetic to your feelings provides a kind of corrective experience. It is validation that you may never have experienced before and that can help you be attuned to and move past your pain.[1]

Demonstrating Self-Compassionate Wisdom

Wisdom belongs to the self-soothing part of self-compassion and

- directs thoughts to yourself that support and guide you,

- provides your child logic with a reality check,

- reminds you that mistakes are a part of being human and helps you learn and grow,

- enables you to consider other possibilities when forming conclusions and adjusting your expectations, and

- originates not only from your past experiences and observations but also from self-awareness based on mindfulness.

To nurture self-compassionate wisdom, you'll need to choose a voice of authority that guides and judges you with compassion. Compassion-focused theory offers a variety of practices to achieve this goal.

Compassion-Focused Theory and Your Compassionate Self

The practices derived from compassion-focused theory stem from studies showing that compassionate feelings and thoughts can physically affect your body to create a sense of safety, calm, connection, and caring.[2] This happens in part due to a release of the hormone oxytocin, which dampens anger arousal. Oxytocin also reduces stress and irritability.[3] Physical contact between loving partners, for example, increases the release of oxytocin, providing a sense of closeness.[4] Oxytocin is also associated with increased trust.[5]

Additionally, researchers have used neuroimaging to identify areas of the brain activated when we mindfully direct compassion toward ourselves or others. One study presented individuals with two different scenarios and instructed them to imagine being either self-critical or self-reassuring.[6] Self-reassurance stimulated the same area of the brain that's triggered when showing compassion and empathy to others.

Recent research suggests that evoking compassion activates the vagus nerve, which creates calmness.[7,8] This nerve stretches from the top of the spine to the organs in the chest, abdomen, and pelvis. It helps coordinate breathing, heart rate, and digestion. Promoting a sense of safety and serenity within yourself reduces the tension of perceived threats and negative feelings such as anger.

The Power of Imagery to Cultivate Self-Compassion

Imagery—the visualization of real or imagined experiences—is known to promote both emotional and physical well-being. Seeing and sensing the details of a scene in your head is a major technique of relaxation exercises and stress management.[9]

We vary in the degree to which we can visualize. Our abilities depend on a lifetime of practice (for help in enhancing this skill, see item 2 of the For Further Reflection section at the end of this chapter). Many of us engage in visualization daily, sometimes without being fully aware of it. We may occasionally picture our lives in the future. At other times, we see moments from our past. Or, we may envision ourselves in ways that are completely based on fantasy.

We can use our visualization skills to expand our self-compassion. The very act of envisioning past and new experiences of compassion can help you make it a dominant force in how you relate to yourself. And evoking memories from past experiences of compassion can expand your mindfulness to consciously show compassion to yourself and others. It's important to remember that visualizing doesn't mean you see a perfectly clear and defined image in your mind. The image is often vague or fleeting.

Exercises for Cultivating Self-Compassion

The following exercises should help you access and expand your compassionate self. You may experience discomfort when first performing them. You can always take a break to practice relaxation or to visualize your safe and peaceful place (see chapter 6 for guidelines on each of these practices), and then resume the exercises when you're more at ease.

Engage in mindfulness breathing for a few minutes before beginning each one. This will expand your immediate ability to observe and be fully present with your experience.

EXERCISE

Connecting with and Expanding Your Compassionate Self

This first exercise was developed by the founder of compassion-focused therapy, Paul Gilbert.[10]

Find a quiet place where you can sit comfortably and undisturbed. Close your eyes if you prefer.

Recall and visualize an experience during which you demonstrated compassion—toward others or yourself. If you can't remember such a moment, imagine yourself demonstrating compassion instead.

Make this experience come alive in your head. Be mindful of how it feels to demonstrate compassion—and savor every part of it. Notice your facial expression, tone of voice, posture, and the inner calm you experience while being compassionate. Picture and feel your face relaxing. Be fully present with the sensations in your body as you envision offering compassion. Observe your breathing and what it feels like in your chest when you are compassionate.

At this moment, you're connecting with that part of you that can be compassionate—warm, nurturing, kind, wise, and nonjudgmental. Take a few minutes to sit with this experience. Then gently open your eyes.

Receiving Compassion and Generating Your Compassionate Self

This is an exercise I have practiced with clients that is based on the principles identified by Paul Gilbert.

First, search your mind for any examples of compassion that you've ever experienced or observed. These may come from real-life experience or from movies, books, or the news. You may also draw on examples from religious or spiritual leaders. Perhaps you envision the Dalai Lama, or Yoda, the Jedi Master in *Star Wars* known for his legendary wisdom, or a most loving and forgiving God. You may even recall compassionate animals or characters from cartoons or comic strips.

Try to identify individuals or characters who have demonstrated, in the most intense way, the qualities that reflect compassion. For example, I remember my seventh-grade social studies teacher, who made time to meet with students after school to discuss classwork, politics, or any concerns we had. I remember him most for his gentleness, openness, and nonjudgmental attitude. I also recall a movie character that, to my mind, is one of the most compassionate people depicted on film. Atticus Finch, played by Gregory Peck in *To Kill a Mockingbird*, exuded consistent and overriding compassion for his children, for those around him, and especially for the person he represented so well in court, a black man accused of rape.

Now, find a place where you can sit without being disturbed. Gently close your eyes if it makes you more comfortable.

Imagine yourself seated in a circle with all of the people, characters, or entities that you've identified. Slowly look around the entire group, paying special attention to each member's facial expression.

Notice the warmth in their eyes or the relaxation in their faces. Observe their postures and general demeanors. For each one, identify the specific aspect of compassion that led you to include him or her in the group. Perhaps it's kindness, wisdom, confidence, nonjudgment, or a sense of connection you feel to them.

Now, imagine your compassionate self as described in the previous exercise. Savor this experience for a few moments, once again noticing your posture, facial expression, and what it feels like in your body when you are compassionate. Especially note your breathing and what it feels like in your chest.

Redirect your attention to the members of your group and picture them showing compassion toward you. Mindfully imagine receiving compassion as each participant might express it. They may show compassion simply in their facial expressions and posture or through their words. Note the sounds of their voices. Perhaps you picture them coming over to you and demonstrating compassion through a hug or a handshake.

Imagine their compassion as positive energy directed at you and merging with the compassionate energy of your compassionate self. Imagine yourself taking in compassionate energy with every inhalation of breath. Feel this capacity for compassion permeating your core, around your heart, in your mind, and throughout your body. Be attentive to making their compassion a part of who you are and who you wish to become. Sit and savor the experience.

Just sit for a moment, sensing the calmness, warmth, and empowerment flow through your body. This is what it feels like to exude compassion and connect with your compassionate self. You've evoked the part of you that's capable of kindness, empathy, sympathy, wisdom, and a powerful connection with yourself and others. Savor this experience for several minutes. Then slowly open your eyes.

My clients say this is a very powerful exercise that increases their mindfulness of specific examples of compassion and unlocks their compassionate selves. They find it very helpful for instilling a sense of calmness and safety within themselves, making them less vulnerable to experiencing anger or acting it out when it does arise. Calmness and safety replace threatening feelings and allow wisdom—and not emotions—to prevail in thoughts and behaviors.

While this exercise can be very positive, some find it unsettling. It may bring up intense feelings of loss as well as thwarted longings for compassion. You may want to engage in relaxing activities before beginning this exercise. And a word of caution: if you experience intense discomfort, you may want to find a therapist who can support you during this exercise.

EXERCISE

Preparing for a Role as a Compassionate Parent in a Play

Most of us have some acting experience, whether playing pretend as a child or in a school program. We drew on knowledge, experience, empathy, and wisdom to think and behave as if we were someone else.

As usual, find a place where you can sit comfortably without any disturbances. Imagine you're assuming the role of a compassionate parent in a play. You'll be asked to show compassion to a child throughout the play, as well as when the child shares intense emotional pain with you.

Think about various models that you can base your acting on. Invoke your compassionate self to play this role. You may choose to use some of the examples from the previous exercise. Identify any phrases, attitudes, and behaviors that you believe are appropriate for a compassionate parent. Whether or not you are a parent, mindfully draw on past experiences and recall the qualities that you associate with compassionate parenting. Gently open your eyes.

How comfortable were you as you played this role? Did you surprise yourself? What qualities did you exhibit that showed compassion? Did this exercise help you connect with your compassionate self? Did you find yourself wanting to fix the child's concern? Were you able to just sit and be with the child during his or her difficult time?

Did any thoughts undermine your attempts to act this role? If possible, use mindfulness to acknowledge them during the exercise and gently redirect your attention to your visualization.

EXERCISE

Envisioning Yourself through the Eyes of Your Older Self

This exercise usually arouses a smile and, at times, slight discomfort. It often leads to a rapid shift in perspective—a new, more mindful way of seeing things.

Envision yourself at ninety years old, with all the life experiences and the wisdom you'll have gained by then. Create an image of your older self—one you can keep returning to—as a person who appears accepting, wise, nurturing, and warm.

With repeated practice, this image of yourself, possessing all of the qualities of self-compassion, will solidify. The more you envision it, the more you'll be able to access this part of yourself when facing the suffering that arouses anger and other negative feelings.

* * *

This chapter has offered strategies to help you evoke and strengthen your compassionate self. Chapter 11 will support you in doing so when experiencing anger arousal.

For Further Reflection

1. I encourage you to complete the Self-Compassion Inventory to determine your current baseline for self-compassion. This inventory, created by psychologist Kristin Neff, is available on her website at http://self-compassion.org. Complete it periodically as you continue cultivating self-compassion.

2. The ability to visualize very much depends on practice. Harvard psychologist Shelley Carson reported this finding in her powerful and informative book *Your Creative Brain*.[11] Try this exercise, based on several offered in her book: Imagine that you've won a 3,500-square-foot condo overlooking Central Park in New York. It's completely unfurnished—just a space without inner walls. Spend fifteen minutes a day for the next eight weeks envisioning how you'll design your new apartment. Imagine where all of the walls and the furnishings will be. This fun and challenging exercise will surprise you with how quickly it improves your visualization skills.

3. Feeling uneasy with self-compassion can be a major obstacle to strengthening your compassionate self. So take a moment to recall any discomfort you experienced while doing the exercises in this chapter. Can you identify any uncomfortable thoughts or feelings? Take a moment to engage in mindfulness breathing. Intentionally recall the negative thought. Then return to your breathing. Or, write your challenging thoughts down and then, if you can, create alternative self-compassionate thoughts. The remaining chapters contain more strategies to deal with this discomfort.

CHAPTER 6

Mindfulness and Self-Compassion for Your Body

Our bodies are the source of our emotions and feelings. According to psychoanalyst Alice Miller, when we ignore the messages of our bodies, they'll still demand to be heard.[1]

Your body moves you toward or away from an experience, whether it's happening within or around you. Being keenly attuned to your body keeps you aware of your feelings, needs, and desires. Such attunement helps in satisfying each of the motivational forces identified in chapter 1: seeking and maintaining safety, promoting warmth and connection, and striving for life fulfillment.

You lose touch with your authentic self when you lack awareness of your body. You disconnect from your true feelings and fail to recognize your most meaningful drives and desires. This makes you more vulnerable to anger.

Body Awareness as a Pathway to Emotional Awareness

Body awareness means showing kindness and concern for your physical well-being, whether you're feeling well or under the weather. Listening to your body grounds you in an experience and enables you to observe rather than react to the experience. Such listening is essential to practicing healthy anger.

We all differ in our openness to noting sensations in our bodies. This can make it especially difficult to recognize our physical reactions to anger.

Such mindfulness requires you to know the exact nature and location of specific sensations. You must truly listen to your body for angry messages. Some people are keenly aware of a pervasive tension throughout their body. Others experience local tension in their arms, face, or chest. And some quickly recognize an increased heart and breathing rate.

When you're angry, you may breathe shallowly, feel your face or arms warm up, or blush. You may perspire more. Many ignore these sensations unless reminded that such reactions to anger are common.

It's no surprise that some people are as out of touch with their bodies as they are with their emotions. Both stem from inhibited self-reflection and self-awareness. Just as we may have learned to ignore our feelings, we may have learned to ignore physical discomfort. We may associate pain tolerance with strength of character, whether modeled by parents, siblings, or the heroes in the movies or TV shows we grew up with. This attitude can be as true for women as it is for men.

Many people disregard the physical symptoms of illness until they grow serious. Some people are passive about their bodies. This attitude can leave someone feeling like an observer who is powerless to alter the course of his or her symptoms.

While growing up, I regularly saw my father deal with arthritis pain in his hands and shoulders. My brother and I suggested that he perform exercises, such as squeezing a rubber ball, to help. But, unable to evoke self-compassion, my father looked at his hands with a sense of disappointment and detachment. His facial expression suggested that he viewed his hands and shoulders as parts of his body over which he had no control—almost as if they belonged to someone else. Sadly, many people relate to their bodies this way.

Being mindful of your body with regard to healthy anger means recognizing even the early stirrings of tension or pain. This promotes increased self-awareness, which helps disrupt and derail your anger.

The exercises in this chapter can help heighten your body awareness. You can practice some of these skills in advance and some during anger arousal. As is true for many people, you may prefer to perform these exercises when someone guides you through them first. You can obtain various CDs and recordings from the Internet that offer guided exercises (see the Resources section).

Getting comfortable with directing yourself in the exercises can make you feel empowered. You're playing an active role in your self-compassion.

EXERCISE

Full Body Scan

This exercise teaches you how to slowly shift your attention over your entire body with compassion and concern for your well-being. It includes elements from exercises developed by Jon Kabat-Zinn, creator of the Mindfulness Based Stress Reduction Program and author of numerous books about mindfulness,[2] and Christopher Germer, psychologist and author of *The Mindful Path to Self-Compassion*.[3]

Wearing comfortable, loose-fitting clothing, find a quiet and comfortable place where you won't be disturbed. Lie down on your bed or on a rug or mat on the floor. Gently close your eyes.

Take a few minutes to practice mindfulness breathing.

Now open your attention to the sensations in your body. This isn't the time to relax but the time to become aware of each sensation. Note the feeling in the muscles of your abdomen as you inhale and exhale. Note the rise and fall of your belly.

Shift your focus to the sensations of pressure where your body contacts the floor or mattress. Linger on them for a moment.

Observe any sensations inside your head. Hold your attention there for a moment. Then focus on the muscles around your eyes and temples. Without moving them, sense whether the muscles are relaxed or tense. At any time, you can switch back to your breathing to refocus.

Shift your attention to the sides of your head, around your ears, for a moment, before focusing on the muscles of your upper and then your lower jaw. Slowly notice the sensations around your nose, cheeks, or mouth. Observe any sensations inside your mouth, in your throat, or on your tongue. With each observation, be sensitive to tension or relaxation. Once again, notice the sensations of your breathing as air enters and exits your body.

Gradually shift your focus to your neck and shoulders, noticing how relaxed or tense they feel. Focus on your upper arms, both front and back, for a moment. Then scan your lower arms, both front and back.

Now focus on your hands—the palms as well as the backs of your hands and your fingers. Notice any sensations on their surface or within.

Slowly scan your upper back and then your lower back, your chest, and your abdomen. Hold your attention on each area for a while. Then observe any sensations within your upper body, your chest, or your abdominal area. Again, notice the movement of your abdomen as you engage each breath.

Move down your body. Notice your lower torso, front and back. Note again how relaxed or tense the surfaces or inside areas feel.

Shift your attention to your upper legs, front and back. Hold your attention there for a moment. Then direct it to your lower legs, front and back.

Move your focus to your feet and toes. Feel whether the muscles in this area are tense or relaxed. Sense the feeling of your toes where they touch each other.

When you've fully scanned your entire body, briefly scan it once again. This time, note any area that feels especially tense. Sit with that tension and linger for a moment, noting how it feels, the space it occupies, and its intensity.

Practice mindfulness breathing for a few moments.

Practicing Body Awareness throughout the Day

You can foster mindfulness of and sensitivity to your body through informal activities as well as the exercises described in this chapter.

Doing a "body check-in" (a brief body scan), as opposed to a full body scan, a few times each day can quickly increase your mindfulness of your body. I would try this midmorning, lunchtime, midafternoon, and at the end of the day.

Simply take a moment to stop whatever you're doing. Breathe deeply and scan your body. Notice any tension, especially around your neck and shoulders. Take a moment to explore and identify the message your body is sending through this tension.

Exercises to Relax and Increase Mindfulness of Your Body

EXERCISE

Visualize Your Muscles Relaxing

Your ability to voluntarily relax your body is fundamental to practicing healthy anger. It aids in self-reflection, allowing your rational mind to better assess and respond to threats.

Whereas mindfulness practice emphasizes observation, the following exercise encourages you to take both an active and an observing role. Practice it when you're relatively calm, and it will serve as a rehearsal for those moments when you're angry. This exercise is powerful because simply visualizing your muscles relaxing can cause them to relax. You'll slowly become more aware of what muscles feel like when they're relaxed or tense.

Playing a sport or a musical instrument well requires careful attention to the way your body moves. You must analyze your movements and adjust as needed. In a like manner, this exercise requires you to be sensitive to the shifts in your body. Practicing this exercise will create a *visceral memory*, a body awareness that becomes easier each time you practice it. Through repetition, your ability to summon physical calmness will become routine.

Wearing comfortable, loose-fitting clothing, find a quiet place to sit or lie down. Gently close your eyes and spend a few minutes engaged in mindfulness breathing.

Picture and feel the muscles of your forehead stretch slightly and release tension, as if the muscle fibers are saying, "Aaaaaah." Shift your attention to the muscles around your eyes and temples as you picture and feel them stretch and relax, releasing tension.

Now, picture and feel the muscles of your upper jaw stretching slightly as they relax and release tension. Shift your attention to your lower jaw and stretch the muscles in that area ever so slightly. Picture and feel them relaxing and releasing tension. You may even want to lower your jaw and move it slightly side to side for further relaxation.

Now focus on the muscles at the back of your neck. Picture and feel them stretch slightly, relaxing and releasing tension. Picture and feel the muscles across your shoulders stretching slightly, relaxing and releasing tension.

Focus on the muscles of your upper arms, front and back. Picture and feel them stretch slightly. Picture and feel them relaxing and releasing tension. Let the muscles of your lower arms, front and back, stretch slightly as you picture and feel them relaxing and releasing tension.

Now picture and feel the finer muscles of your hands and fingers stretch slightly, relaxing and releasing tension.

Picture and feel the muscles of your upper back stretching slightly, relaxing and releasing tension. Picture and feel the muscles of your lower back stretching slightly, relaxing and releasing tension.

Picture and feel the muscles of your chest stretching slightly, relaxing and releasing tension. Now picture and feel the muscles of your abdomen stretching slightly, relaxing and releasing tension.

Picture and feel the muscles of your lower torso, front and back, stretching slightly, relaxing and releasing tension.

Picture and feel the muscles of your upper legs, front and back, stretching slightly, relaxing and releasing tension.

Picture and feel the muscles of your lower legs, front and back, stretching slightly, relaxing and releasing tension.

Picture and feel the finer muscles of your feet and toes stretching out ever so slightly, relaxing and releasing tension.

At this point, scan your body, being mindful of any area that feels especially tense. Focus your attention there and imagine that, like a cube of sugar in a cup of hot tea, it's dissolving and disappearing so that your entire body remains completely calm.

Now, to heighten your awareness of how calm you are, shift your attention to the muscles of your forehead and note how relaxed they feel. Scan the muscles around your eyes and temples and note how relaxed they feel. Note the muscles of your jaw and how relaxed they feel. Note how relaxed the muscles in the back of your neck and across your shoulders feel. Note the muscles of your upper arms, front and back, and how relaxed they feel. Notice the muscles of your lower arms, front and back, and how relaxed they feel. Observe the finer muscles of your hands and fingers and how relaxed they feel. Notice how relaxed the muscles feel in your upper and lower back. Observe how relaxed the muscles feel across your chest and abdomen. Note the muscles of your lower torso and how relaxed they feel. Note the muscles of your upper legs, front and back, and how relaxed they feel. Note the muscles of your lower legs and how relaxed they feel. And, finally, notice the finer muscles of your feet and toes and how relaxed they feel.

At this moment, your entire body is completely relaxed. It probably feels warmer and maybe a little heavier than when you began this exercise. This is what it feels like to be fully relaxed. Be mindful of how this feels.

Think about whether you experienced any discomfort while doing this exercise. Some people become tense, while others feel uneasy with being so relaxed. This may be the case if you tend to have Type A personality traits, such as an overly intense drive to achieve. You may be extremely concerned with your use of time and view just sitting still as a waste of it. Understandably, this will lead you to experience great tension.

Some people who experience distress during this exercise report a great deal of tension in their past. This may have resulted from physical or emotional abuse. Victims of such experiences feel threatened more easily. Understandably, they may resist relaxing, as if letting down their guard makes them once again vulnerable to harm.

I've often referred to this ongoing state of apprehension as *prairie dog syndrome*. No, this isn't a diagnosis recognized by any professional group. But I believe the image of a prairie dog standing on its hind legs, frantically alert for any hint of danger, represents this tendency well.

My friend John shared some experiences that call the prairie dog syndrome to mind. John is a napropath, a health care provider trained in alternative medicine and manipulative therapies. He treats neuromusculo-skeletal conditions—connective tissue disorders that might, for example, affect the spinal column and joints. John usually plays background music in his office. He said it's not uncommon for some of his clients to ask him to turn the music off. It relaxes them too much, making them uncomfortable. Several of his clients have cried as they settled into a relaxed state.

Therapists who practice body work to deal with emotional conflicts are well aware of how the body affects our thoughts and feelings. This often occurs without our conscious awareness. Feeling uneasy about self-compassion may also contribute to tension during a relaxation exercise. The more you work at cultivating self-compassion, the more open you'll be to relaxing your body.

EXERCISE

Progressive Relaxation

Progressive muscle relaxation, developed by Herbert Benson, a cardiologist and founder of the Benson-Henry Institute for Mind Body Medicine at Massachusetts General Hospital, is one of the most highly recommended ways to achieve physical calm.[4] It involves alternately tensing and relaxing muscle groups. The following exercise uses this approach.

This exercise should enhance your ability to distinguish between relaxed and tense muscles. It will help you become more mindful of how muscles feel when they transition from relaxed to tense, and vice versa. Mindfulness, just one aspect of self-compassion, will help you notice subtle differences in muscle tone, especially as physical tension gradually rises during anger arousal.

Find a place where you can sit comfortably, undisturbed, for about fifteen minutes. For this exercise, it will be helpful to sit in a chair that has arms. Repeat each of the following steps three times.

Begin by tightening the muscles around your eyes and holding them in that position for a moment (don't do this if you wear contacts). Notice the tension and how it feels. Now gradually relax the muscles. Be mindful of how they feel as you release the tension and fully relax.

Now clench your teeth and observe the muscle tension in your jaws as you do so. Push your tongue against the roof of your mouth. Hold it for a few seconds before gradually lowering your tongue and lower jaw as you observe the feeling of the muscles relaxing.

Raise and hold your shoulders as close to your ears as you can. Keep that position for a few seconds while you focus on the tension. Then gradually lower your shoulders and notice how relaxed they become. You may want to lower them slightly below their starting position to relax them even further.

Pushing your elbows down against the arms of your chair, tighten the muscles of your upper arms and note the tension. Hold them in place for a few seconds before relaxing.

Push your forearms down on the arms of the chair. Observe the tension as you hold them in place for several seconds. Relax and note the feeling.

Now clench your fists and focus on the muscle tension in your hands and fingers. After holding this position for a few seconds, slowly open your fingers and hands and notice how the muscles feel as they relax.

Pull in your abdomen, as if you're trying to touch your navel to your spine. Notice the tension. Then pay attention to how these muscles feel as you gradually relax.

Tighten the muscles of your lower torso. Note their tension as you hold them in place for several seconds. Then relax and observe the feeling.

Sitting straight, press your feet flat against the floor as you push your knees together and tighten your thighs. Hold that position momentarily. Notice how relaxed they feel as you gradually release the tension.

Stretch your legs in front of you, with your heels touching the floor. Raise, point, and move your toes toward you as you stretch the back muscles of your lower legs. Feel the tension, followed by the relaxed feeling as you release them.

Now, stretch your legs in front of you with your toes pointed away from you and feel the tension in your front leg muscles. Hold them in place for several seconds and then relax.

Finally, curl your toes until they tense and then relax, noticing how they feel.

Now, scan your body from your head to your toes and notice how relaxed it can be.

EXERCISE

Deep Breathing

Your breathing becomes shallower when you grow angry. This is because of the physical tension that accompanies feeling threatened. It serves as an important cue to pay attention to your body. As soon as you recognize this tension, begin your mindfulness breathing, with a special focus on deep breathing. It's a powerful way to connect with your body and rapidly feel calmer.

First, slowly and deeply inhale. Focus specifically on deep breathing, which moves the diaphragm. Hold it for a second. While picturing your navel touching your spine, exhale from the deepest part of your lungs and pull in your abdomen. Do this slowly three to four times and then engage in mindfulness breathing for several minutes.

Deep breathing is one of the quickest ways to listen to the message your anger is telling you.

EXERCISE

Your Peaceful Place

This exercise helps you create imagery to achieve calmness and safety.

Again, find a place where you can sit comfortably without being disturbed for about fifteen minutes. Gently close your eyes.

Picture a place where you've been or would like to be—a place where you feel safe, relaxed, peaceful, and content. Use your imagination to make the scene as real as possible. Imagine yourself there. You may find your mind wandering at times. That's all right. Just redirect your attention to your scene. As you envision this place, observe its colors, light, and shadows.

Notice the air around you. Imagine how it feels on your face and hands. Is it dry or humid? Is it moving or still? Try to make this place real. Does this very safe and peaceful place have a smell? Inhale deeply to imagine any fragrance that's part of the scene.

Observe any sounds that occur in your safe, comfortable, and peaceful place. Or, imagine the stillness if it's quiet. Observe the objects in your scene. Notice their colors and their shapes. Notice their lines. Are they straight or curved? Are the objects circular, square, rectangular, or irregular? Now picture the objects and pay attention to how they might feel. One may be smooth and another rough. Imagine all of the different parts of your scene.

Now envision yourself reaching out and touching one of the objects in this setting. Notice its colors, texture, and lines or curves. Feel it in your hand. This is just one of many objects making this a peaceful, safe, and relaxing place.

If you haven't yet done so, find a place to sit in your very peaceful and safe place. Shift your attention from your scene to your body. Watch your chest and notice how relaxed your breathing is. Notice how relaxed the muscles in your face, neck, and shoulders feel. Observe your arms but don't move them. Just note how relaxed they feel. Now notice your belly, arms, hands, torso, and legs and how relaxed they feel. Enjoy this relaxed and safe feeling for a moment.

Return your focus to your peaceful scene. Observe your scene using all of your senses, once again noting the colors, shapes, air, scents, and sounds—everything that makes your scene safe and peaceful. Do this for a few minutes and then gradually open your eyes.

Many guided meditations are available that focus on peaceful places (see Resources section). You may wish to locate one that evokes the scene you just imagined.

The Power of Visual Imagery

Your body responds to what you envision. The self-compassion exercises described in chapter 5 show this clearly. Practicing visualization can have a powerful calming effect, especially during anger arousal.

Suppose, for example, that a careless driver abruptly cuts in front of you. You may choose to picture that driver as a five-year-old possessing his or her adult head. This image evokes laughter—or at least a smile—every time I suggest it. Visualizing a funny image causes a reaction in your body that overrides anger. It's hard for these two emotions to exist simultaneously in your body. Clearly, visualization can quickly keep anger from escalating.

Intense anger can lead you to view certain people as wicked and evil. Picturing past experiences that show their more positive, caring, or compassionate side can help avoid this. This technique isn't meant to deny or minimize your anger. It's to help you rationally and constructively manage your anger so that you are sufficiently calm to consider the reasons behind a person's behavior.

A client I worked with several years ago provided a good example of the power of visualization. Rachel, a veterinarian, was excited that after many years of planning, she was finally able to open her own clinic. But she faced a major difficulty: whenever she entered the waiting room, she became extremely stressed—not by the animals waiting to see her but by their owners. She saw them as demanding, anxious, entitled, and, at times, verbally aggressive.

I suggested she visualize her human clients as impatient children who are fearful about their pets' ailments or injuries. I told her to picture each person, whether he or she held a cat, dog, rabbit, or parakeet, as driven by child logic in a moment of feeling threatened. This image helped Rachel become empathetic. She realized that their actions stemmed from a shared concern: the desire for immediate and quality care for their beloved animals. Visualization used this way can effectively achieve a sense of safety and calmness.

Listening to Music

Listening to music is another way to help you relax. It may not soothe you as deeply as the other exercises, but researchers have found that listening to music reduces the levels of cortisol in the body.[5] Although some studies suggest classical music for this, you should use whatever genre relaxes you the most.[6]

Music can echo our deepest emotions or lead us away from those emotions. While some people readily react to music's calming impact, others may need to practice a bit.

*   *   *

By expanding mindfulness of your body, you gain increased access to and awareness of your feelings as well as your thoughts. Being able to relax your body as you do this helps you to achieve the sense of safety that is needed for flexible self-reflection. The framework of anger described in the next chapter provides guidelines for this reflection.

For Further Reflection

1. What was your experience like while reading this chapter? Did the content or exercises trigger any specific feelings, thoughts, or bodily reactions? Were you tense? Were you critical of the suggestions? Did you complete all the exercises? If not, what did you tell yourself about practicing them? Did you prefer certain exercises over others? If so, why?

2. Did you experience any of the challenges described in chapter 2 while reading this chapter? If so, which ones? Do any of your thoughts discourage you from paying attention to your body? Perhaps you feel self-absorbed or that you're wasting precious time by taking part in these practices.

3. Reducing your quickness to anger may convince you that you don't need to make these exercises a priority. Developing body memory, however, depends on repetition. So, how can you encourage yourself to do these exercises when you believe you don't need them?

4. Be mindful of how these skills can help you manage negative emotions. Be attentive to your body when you're experiencing both negative and positive feelings.

CHAPTER 7

A Framework for Understanding Anger

When practiced together, mindfulness and self-compassion skills "reduce reactivity, strengthen autonomy, promote emotional sensitivity, enhance understanding of historical sources of our hurts, and provide guidelines for safe, effective communication."[1] Both approaches give us the freedom to choose how to react to our anger. But there are other self-awareness skills that let us look deeply into each experience and further our capacity for healthy anger.

Self-awareness skills will help you explore how your anger relates to your desires, needs, and expectations. They can teach you to distinguish among your emotions. You'll learn to be mindful of the way your thoughts, feelings, and reactions interact to trigger anger. As psychologist Paul Ekman says, "To have a choice about how you are going to enact an emotion, you must be aware of the emotion as it is arising, of the 'spark before the flame' . . . the impulse before the action."[2]

The framework in this chapter will help you develop such awareness. It uses a model that I've presented to clients and workshop participants for more than twenty years.[3]

Just as a magnifying glass shows details that are invisible to the naked eye, this framework will reveal what forms the spark of your anger arousal. Knowing this can make you more mindful about reducing your vulnerability to anger.

The framework requires you to develop both mindfulness and self-compassion skills. However, it goes beyond just being mindful of the moment you first feel anger. Rather, it can help you be mindful of a series of moments—internal experiences—and how they interact.

Rather than start at the beginning of this series of experiences, I'll begin with the endpoint—the moment you first feel anger. Anger is the one emotional experience that you can most clearly and readily recognize.

Anger

When asked to describe an anger-provoking situation, many of us reply that a *triggering event* caused our anger. Figure 7.1 shows a timeline for such an event.

Fig. 7.1

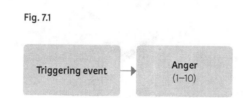

Although most people might answer this way, this explanation isn't very detailed or accurate about what happens when we grow angry. The true sequence is more complex. Several factors play a significant role before a triggering event. Others affect our reactions immediately after a triggering event. And some exert their greatest impact during the exact moment when anger occurs. The framework here identifies these factors and the potential role they can play in anger arousal. The following exercise can help you discover them.

EXERCISE

Identifying the Components of Anger Arousal

Find a comfortable place where you can sit awhile without distractions. Practice mindfulness breathing for a few minutes. Then evoke your compassionate self. Engaging in these practices before the exercise will make you more open and attentive to your observations.

Recall a recent situation during which you became angry. Picture that incident as if it were on a video recording. As best you can, re-create in your mind all aspects of that scenario: the setting, the people, their actions, and your behavior. The goal is to relive your experience as realistically as possible. Just recalling the situation may lead you to experience some discomfort. Select a different situation if necessary.

Picture objects within the scene. Note their color, shape, texture, and composition. If people were involved, try to remember their appearance, clothing, stature, mannerisms, and facial expressions, and the content and tone of anything they said. Recall the time of day and even the weather, if that seems relevant. The closer your mental picture is to your real experience, the more intensely you'll feel your mind-body state from that time.

Now that you've immersed yourself in your past experience, try to be fully mindful about what your anger felt like. Rate your anger on a continuum in which 1 reflects slight irritation and 10 reflects the most severe, intense anger.

Bodily Reactions

Reviewing your "video," pause and think about the moment you felt anger but had yet to act on it. Gradually scan your entire body from head to toe. Before reading any further, pause and observe the range of sensations you experienced just before and during anger arousal.

How did your body react? Did any of your muscles feel tense? If so, was the tension in your arms, chest, or neck, around your eyes, or throughout your body? Did your body temperature rise? Some people feel warmer when they're angry. Did your breathing change in any way? Did it become more rapid and/or shallow than before? These are the most frequently experienced physical responses to anger.

It's possible that you experienced tension only on a general level and can't identify the details of your physical state. Perhaps you simply recall feeling agitated. Figure 7.2 shows the sequences in your anger arousal up to this point.

Fig. 7.2

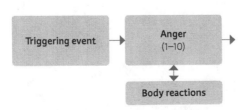

The two-way arrow in this diagram shows that feelings of anger come from the body and that such feelings can cause physical sensations. Your bodily reactions affect your emotions and your emotions fuel your bodily reactions. As explored in chapter 6, recognizing the sensations within your body will help you become aware of your emotions. Your mindfulness toward such sensations allows you to constructively respond to your emotions with self-compassion.

Self-Talk

Now, as best you can, recall any thoughts (or internal dialogue) you may have had during this same moment of anger. This is the "self-talk" that you experienced while angry; it's not necessarily what you would have said aloud to express your anger. Your thoughts may have included complete sentences or simply a phrase or a word. For example, you may have thought: "Damn!" "I'll show you!" "I can't let you get away with this." "I can't believe this is happening." Or, "How unfair!" Figure 7.3 shows this element within the sequence.

Fig. 7.3

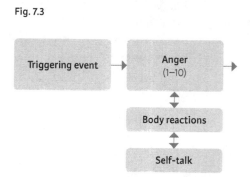

Pondering what you said to yourself while angry is yet another exercise in mindfulness. Suppose, for example, that you became angry after a close friend told someone else a secret that you had shared with her. At the moment you experienced anger, you might have thought one or all of the following: "Jerk!" "Some friend!" "I have to get even." Or, "That's it!"

Internal dialogue at the moment of anger can either heighten your tension or calm it. Practicing healthy anger and self-compassion means knowing whether your thoughts during such moments relieve your suffering or make it worse. By being mindful of such thoughts, you'll soon realize that you can choose your preferred form of self-talk. As such, you can gradually become more attentive to practicing a calming internal dialogue.

Images

Some people see images in their mind during their moment of anger. These may focus on whatever led to the triggering event. Or they may consist of imagined ways of expressing one's anger. Recall whether you experienced any picture in your mind during your moment of anger. Let's return to the example of the friend who broke your trust. At the moment you became enraged, perhaps you evoked an angry image of her—or perhaps even one that depicted a positive interaction that you had with her in the past.

Being mindful of such images, like being mindful of your body or self-talk, allows you to realize the experience is only temporary. It lets you identify alternative images that may be more calming rather than those that incite you to anger. The sequence depicted in figure 7.4 shows an example of this.

Fig. 7.4

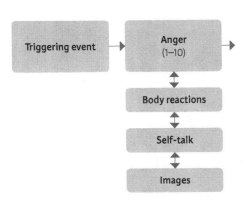

Negative Feelings

Now rewind your "recording" ever so slightly, focusing on the distinct moment leading up to your anger. Try to remember any negative feelings you experienced immediately before you grew angry. As mentioned in chapter 1, anger is often a reaction to or a distraction from these feelings. This is perhaps the most intensely uncomfortable moment in the timeline of anger arousal. It's this moment that catapults you into anger. And it's the moment that calls for self-compassion. To some extent, you may experience these negative feelings because you feel threatened. In fact, by doing this exercise, you may feel threatened by experiencing them once again.

You may find it challenging to identify these feelings at first. You may have found them so uncomfortable that you quickly removed them from your awareness.

It's understandable that, like many people engaging in this exercise for the first time, you might name *annoyed, irritated,* or *resentful* as some of the negative feelings that preceded your anger. These words, however, simply describe variations of anger. Or, you may say you felt *agitated,* a word that focuses on your physical state rather than your feelings. It's important to remember that being able to differentiate your emotions weakens the relationship between anger and aggression.[4] And your ability to recognize your feelings as they occur is a key factor of *emotional intelligence.*[5] Other components of emotional intelligence include the ability to distinguish among your feelings and to recognize and distinguish feelings in others. Emotional intelligence furthers your connection with yourself and with others, enriching your relationships and helping you achieve your goals.

Take a moment to engage in mindfulness breathing and then resume mindfully focusing your attention on identifying the feelings you felt just prior to growing angry. Some might include:

sadness	depression
disappointment	confusion
shame	rejection
embarrassment	feeling ignored
frustration	feeling devalued

Usually, anger is a reaction to more than one negative emotion. You may find that you react to one or more of these feelings. Figure 7.5 illustrates this moment in the anger experience. This diagram, which shows that bodily reactions, self-talk, and images may accompany negative feelings, also includes examples of negative feelings. It highlights the fact that any feelings you experience are always a part of your general mind-body state. And, again, the arrows point in both directions to show how these factors can influence one another.

In reviewing your scenario, try to remember whether you berated yourself for becoming angry. Did you become anxious about becoming angry?

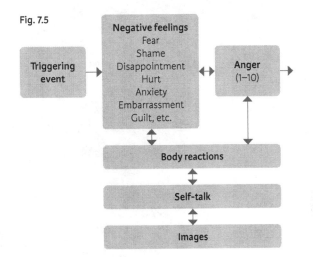

Fig. 7.5

Or, perhaps you felt embarrassment or even shame. Maybe you just felt disappointment. Judging yourself for your anger or the feelings that preceded it may produce these negative emotions. This only intensifies anger arousal.

Appraisal

An *appraisal* is a knee-jerk reaction, a form of self-talk that may occur so rapidly and quietly that you remain unaware of it. In essence, appraisals are the first thoughts you make about the event. Gaining awareness of your immediate, knee-jerk appraisals is a significant step toward understanding how your thoughts contribute to the feelings (including threat) that provoke anger. Figure 7.6 shows the framework for anger that includes the appraisals.

Having identified the feelings that fueled your anger, take a moment to mindfully remember the instant the triggering event registered in your awareness. Can you identify the appraisals you formed that triggered your negative feelings?

In the scenario with your close friend, knee-jerk thoughts may include: "She betrayed me." "I can't believe it." "I knew I shouldn't have trusted her." "Now, I'll lose the friendship of the person she told the secret to." "She really embarrassed me." "I can't trust anyone." Or, "I was a fool to tell her." Clearly, some of these thoughts may lead to the feelings identified in figure 7.6.

Fig. 7.6

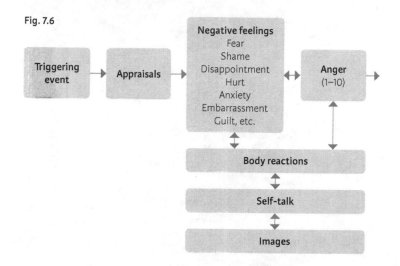

Appraisals may be unrealistic. They're often overly influenced by child logic instead of more rational thought. They usually occur so quickly that we fail to be mindful of them. And yet, they may reveal how we usually respond to such situations. Our habits can make us more vulnerable to negative feelings and close our minds to alternative appraisals. Some very general and unrealistic appraisals include but aren't limited to:

- The event proves he or she doesn't like or care about me. (This was most likely not the case.)
- The event occurred because of something I did. (This was most likely not the case.)
- He (she) purposely did something to annoy me. (This was most likely not the case.)
- That event proves the world isn't safe at all.
- People don't care.
- If this happened, there can't be a God.
- If my partner (or child, parent, etc.) did that, he (she) doesn't love me.
- My entire self-regard depends on this one event (achieving a specific goal, having a specific skill or physical attribute, etc.).
- My entire future rests on this one event (even when it doesn't).

- If this happened, it means I shouldn't have done what I did.

- If this occurred, none of my needs, desires, or expectations will be satisfied.

- Since this happened and my expectations weren't satisfied, I'll never be able to satisfy my needs or desires in any other way.

- I might as well give up.

- I have no control over my life.

These examples may not exactly depict your particular appraisal, but they show how you might react when things don't go the way you want them to. To some extent, your reactions may stem from an *emotional script* rooted in your childhood and adolescence that may narrow the ways in which you see your world—habitually sensitive to certain details while ignoring others.[6] Living according to this script is intended to keep you safe. It can become overly protective, however, making you vulnerable to feeling that the satisfaction of your needs and desires is threatened when no threat exists. Often, overly intense reactions can be traced to the past— and not just with regard to the triggering event. This past can consist of the seconds, minutes, hours, days, or even weeks leading up to an event. It could also include recent years or the very early years of your life. For example, a person may experience the most recent situation as just another reminder of similar but much more painful experiences. Such experiences shape the patterns in a person's neural pathways and leave him or her vulnerable to anger.

The current triggering event may be seen as just another roadblock in a long history of unmet needs, desires, or expectations. It's common for people to have a *hot button*—a pattern of thinking or feeling influenced by past experiences and genetics—that makes them overly sensitive and quick to anger at certain times. Cheryl, age thirty-three, offers an example of this when describing her anger toward Jeff, her boyfriend of two years:

> I became enraged when he didn't come home on time, didn't keep his word to call me on time, or spent what I considered to be "too much time" with his friends. I usually quickly concluded that he didn't really love me or that he couldn't be trusted or that he was being totally unfair.

Much of Cheryl's anger stemmed from fears and anxieties about being abandoned, an insecurity from her past. Her two prior long-term relationships ended when her boyfriends left. Cheryl's parents divorced when she was six years old. Her mother dated many men and remarried when Cheryl was thirteen. Her mother's poor self-esteem and constant string of relationships made her less available for Cheryl.

Cheryl's current relationship woke many of those old feelings. Negative feelings and attitudes toward others and herself were rekindled the moment she entered an intimate relationship. This included her anger, expressed by demeaning accusations against her boyfriend.

To some degree, Jeff's behavior contributed to Cheryl's sensitivity. His untreated attention deficit disorder made it difficult for him to be punctual.

By practicing mindfulness and using this model, Cheryl gradually realized that a variety of factors, including her past history and self-esteem, influenced her appraisals. She realized that when Jeff came home late, she was revisiting anxiety stemming from earlier relationships. She made appraisals about her boyfriend's actions through the eyes of her younger self, a child who felt intense loss, sadness, and insecurity. These recent events were just another reminder that she couldn't expect to depend on others and was unlovable. Her child logic and a sense of helplessness—a part of her mindset throughout her childhood—fueled these issues.

Now suppose that, unlike Cheryl, you're more secure with yourself and have a positive history with people you see as trustworthy. You may be concerned when your partner behaves like her boyfriend, but your emotions may differ in both quality and intensity. You may experience confusion or low-level anxiety, disappointment, or frustration when you don't hear from your partner. Unlike Cheryl, though, you may experience these emotions without feeling threatened. And your anger, if aroused, may be much less intense than it would be if influenced by insecurity, fear of loss, distrust, and poor self-esteem.

Sensitivities differ for everyone. Suppose you came from a family that expressed extreme anxiety about money and financial security. You might overreact to financial concerns as an adult. Like other hot buttons, your past can heighten your emotions and cause you to become inflexible in your thinking. Like children, who are highly sensitive to the emotions of those around them, your child logic may be hypervigilant to possible financial ruin. You may, as an adult, be highly prone to feeling threatened about finances even when such fears aren't warranted. The resulting anxiety may drive your anger, especially when your appraisals lead you to feel powerless about your finances.

Or, you may have an intense need for fairness and be especially quick to believe others are treating you unfairly. Some people are overly sensitized to feeling devalued or abandoned. The more mindful you become about your hot-button sensitivities, the more you'll begin to see how they leave you vulnerable to anger.

Being mindful of your appraisals during anger arousal is an opportunity for you to intervene and alter the course of your anger. Once you identify your appraisals, you must decide which are accurate and realistic and which are overly influenced by past learning and hot-button issues. You'll consider alternative appraisals that are increasingly objective, less inciting, and ultimately more self-compassionate. You'll be "mindful" rather than "mindless" and choose rational appraisals rather than those dominated by child logic.

The Triggering Event

Anger begins with a triggering event that challenges your internal harmony and well-being. It may or may not be due to a person's behavior—for example, lightning strikes a tree that falls on your car, your beloved puppy destroys your favorite pair of shoes, or your computer crashes.

The trigger may be a single event, or it may be just one in a series of events that combine to affect your mood. You may experience a single event as the proverbial "last straw" in a series of trying events.

Suppose, for example, that you're driving to work when you realize that you left your cell phone at home. You return to get your phone, feeling a little tense due to the delay. When you get to work, you log on to your computer and find twenty e-mails requiring your immediate attention. While reviewing these e-mails, your supervisor asks you to attend an emergency meeting. Each of these events alone might not cause a great amount of negative emotion. But taken together, they may leave you feeling overwhelmed. You may experience frustration or anxiety without anger. Due to your built-up frustration, however, the next situation that irritates you may become the target of your anger—especially if you appraise the situation as being unfair, unjustified, and threatening.

Stress makes us more brittle when responding to any new event. This may be the death of a loved one, work demands, the challenges of parenting, an illness or accident, or several of these events occurring in sequence or at the same time.

Even positive events can cause us to become irritable. Evan, aged thirty-two, described a number of pressures he had experienced in the year leading up to his contacting me:

> In June, I graduated with my MBA. I married in July and by the end of August, we'd bought a home. Oh, and I also started a new job in September . . . and two months ago, in December, my wife became pregnant.

While he wasn't necessarily prone to anger in the past, Evan said that his wife and friends noticed that he seemed increasingly irritable. Clearly, while each of these events might be positive on its own, the timing caused Evan tremendous tension. Evan had a long history of needing to please others. This often led him to say yes when he really preferred to say no. His repeated failure to speak up about his feelings of pressure led him to agree to these life changes over a short time. As a result, his stress turned into intense anxiety. It's understandable that he experienced anxiety without anger, even though others saw him as irritable. Because of his need to please, his anger made him very uncomfortable. In fact, a part of his anxiety derived from growing angry at those he loved most. After much reflection, Evan became more comfortable acknowledging his anger. And he soon learned that the freedom to say no is a major part of healthy anger management.

A triggering event may be real or imagined. You might wake up angered by a dream in which your desires were thwarted. You could become angry about an event you imagine or anticipate occurring in the future. Just picturing that event in your mind may coax you into feelings that evolve into anger.

At times, you may remain unaware of how much an event has influenced your anger arousal. This happens more frequently when you direct your anger inward. Sarah, a client I saw several years ago, offers an example of how this plays out. She reported that she had felt increasingly "brittle" as well as "down" in her mood over the course of the week prior to our meeting. At first, she couldn't find the reason for her shift in mood. Further investigation remedied that.

On Monday of that week, Sarah had received negative feedback from her supervisor about a project she'd been working on. She immediately felt diminished and somewhat devalued. As the week progressed, she found herself highly self-critical and doubtful of her ability to do her job. Though she was not mindful of it at the time, her reactions were consistent with how she'd learned to manage her negative emotions, including anger. She described her understanding as follows:

> I grew up very uncomfortable with anger. Neither of my parents ever expressed anger, either in words or in their behavior. And they never had to tell me not to be angry; I just saw how they reacted to my older brother when he became angry. My dad would look at him with a facial expression that clearly showed his hurt and disappointment. I could still picture now how he looked back then. My dad would then withdraw. Sometimes he wouldn't speak to my brother for several days. My mother would never say anything. She just behaved as if nothing had happened. I guess I just resolved to do whatever I could to make sure my dad didn't look at me with his "look." And I never wanted to be the target of his silent treatment.

Sarah had grown up fearful of anger and was ashamed to show anger. She strived to avoid becoming angry or the target of anger. When she became angry with others, she directed that anger at herself. While she was able to recognize and accept feeling anxious and devalued, she wasn't immediately aware of how the event had triggered her anger.

Being alert to the events that trigger anger arousal means being alert to being mindful. Certainly, you may be in a bad mood at times and, in spite of self-reflection, you may remain clueless as to what triggered it. If that's the case, it may be helpful to go back to it later or move on. The more mindful you become of your unique triggers, the better you'll recognize the types of events to which you're most sensitive.

Expectations

Each morning, you wake with a blueprint of expectations of others, the world, and yourself. These expectations are rooted in your past experiences, up to this moment. They revolve around your real needs for survival as well as your perceived needs and desires. They help form your mindset as you confront your day's events.

All your experiences are measured at any given moment on any given day against your expectations. And how you respond to the discrepancy between your expectations and reality makes all the difference. If the events that unfold conform to your expectations as the morning progresses, you'll most likely feel content. If you're fortunate and this continues throughout the day, you go to bed at night and call it a "good" day. You may feel empowered and see the world as receptive and supportive. Most importantly, you feel the safety that fuels your contentment. And while you may not say it, you probably feel that life is good. If only life were so simple.

Figure 7.7 depicts contentment when expectations are satisfied and a variety of negative feelings when they are not.

Our expectations influence every aspect of our lives. Some are realistic and, unfortunately, many are not. We often maintain such expectations without being fully mindful of them.

Fig. 7.7

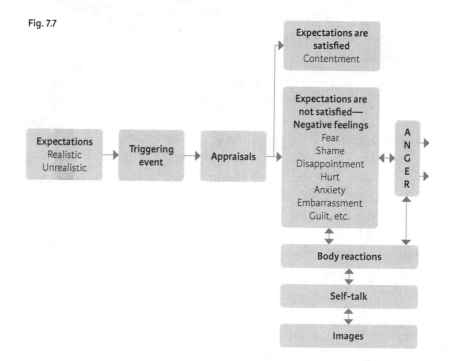

Expectations about Daily Activities

Think about the activities you engage in throughout the day. For example, you may dash into a gas station to buy a sandwich on your lunch break, after getting stuck in traffic while running errands. Suppose that you'd envisioned enjoying a relaxing lunch at a small cafe nearby. You clearly had expectations for how your lunch hour should unfold. How irritated you become will depend on how flexible you are about your expectations.

You expect your commute to take a certain amount of time. You expect that your encounters with people won't be out of the ordinary. You expect that the meal you eat at your favorite restaurant will be as delicious as it has been in the past. You may expect that the news will have nothing startling to report or that the device you read it on will work well.

Each of these expectations influences how you approach the day, even when you're too preoccupied to notice. Taking the orderliness of our universe for granted, unfortunately, leaves us vulnerable to anger.

Expectations in Relationships

Your expectations have an impact on every relationship you form, whether with your family, friends, coworkers, or others. For example, let's return to the anecdote about a friend's betrayal. You may expect a "true" friend to behave a certain way. You may believe that he or she should always take your side when you disagree with others. Perhaps you measure your friends by their availability to help you when you need them. You may think that real friends should never disappoint you, that they should lend you money, that they should help you move, and that they should never, ever date your ex. In an intimate relationship, you may expect your partner to know exactly what you need to feel loved.

We quite often judge others based on how we think they should behave. Everyone experiences such expectations. Take a moment to review your anger-provoking event from earlier. In hindsight, what had you expected from the triggering event? To what degree were your expectations influenced by your emotions? To what extent were your expectations based more on your desires than on your needs?

Expectations and Judgment

You observe a person and think, "I just can't believe it. How could he think that? I can't believe he did that." Such reactions are rooted in your wide variety of expectations regarding the "right" way for people to behave. Such thinking fails to consider that people are different and can and do choose different approaches.

Perhaps you observe a parent scolding a child while in a restaurant. You may immediately think, "What a horrible parent." Or you might just mutter "horrible" under your breath. You may just experience a surge of tension that reflects your anxiety or your disappointment and maybe even disgust with the parent's behavior. Alternatively, you may share the parent's reactions, with thoughts such as "I can't believe that child is behaving that way." Or, "If he was my child, I'd . . ." In each situation, you've made a knee-jerk comparison between how these people behave and how you believe they should behave.

We judge others based on our expectations. These judgments may derive from compassion and empathy. When we're critical of the parent, we may be sympathizing with the child and the pain we assume she's experiencing. In contrast, our criticism of the child may come from identifying with the disrespect, frustration, or powerlessness we believe the parent faces.

Expectations and the Workplace

Just as in personal relationships, reacting less to anger in the workplace depends on being mindful and flexible in our expectations. Sean is a perfect example of this.

Sean worked at a company for thirteen years. During that time, he was highly successful. He rose up through the ranks and attained a middle management position. One day, he went in to work and was told he had three hours to gather his belongings. He would then be escorted out of the building. Sean described his reactions:

> I've been furious! I know this happens. In my mind, it happens to other people. And I was so totally unprepared for it. I mean, I trusted the company, and I trusted my supervisor. That's what makes it even more difficult. I feel so betrayed. I worked so hard over these last few years and gave so much of my time and energy. And then they give me three hours to pack. How unfair . . . and I couldn't do a thing about it.

Sean had heard rumors that his company might merge with another firm. His supervisor had repeatedly assured him that he wouldn't be affected by the change. Little did he know that the new company's management had decided to eliminate his department.

Sean's expectations had formed over many years. His past promotions and praise from his boss convinced him that these expectations would be fulfilled. Based on observing his father and others, Sean expected good work to be rewarded financially and with job security. Unfortunately, Sean learned that job security is much more unpredictable than it used to be. Changes in the workplace are always occurring. This is the new reality.

If you hold on to expectations too tightly, you'll only contribute to your suffering.

Expectations and Attachment

Being aware of your rigid attachments is crucial to understanding how you contribute to your anger. Buddhist writings address this when they describe *attachment* as an exaggerated emotional investment in ideas, people, or material goods.[7] Your attachments may provide you with some degree of structure, harmony, and what you believe to be meaning in your life. Much suffering occurs, however, when you foster overly intense attachments. And the threats to these attachments often form the basis for much of your anger.

For example, when you're overly attached to certain ideas, you fail to remain open-minded or to consider anything that may contradict what you believe. Or, with your overly intense love for your partner, you may not embrace your own path and identity because there's so little room to do so. Similarly, craving possessions—whether your home, your car, or your bank account—may reflect a rigid attachment to things as a way to define your self-worth. In each case, becoming too attached and holding rigid expectations can leave you vulnerable to anger.

Expectations about Life in General

Life is full of challenges. Things happen that are beyond our control. We can only face them as best we can with the resources we possess.

All too often, when confronted by challenges, we may hold on to the belief that life should always go the way we expect it to. It's natural to experience negative feelings when our expectations aren't met. Becoming aware of our expectations helps us realize how they contribute to our anguish.

Examples of Expectations

Psychologist David Burns suggests that when we tenaciously hold on to "shoulds," we're living a "shouldy" life.[8] Expectations dominated by "shoulds" can lead to suffering that is far worse than simply accepting what cannot be. The following unrealistic expectations often fuel anger:

- I should be perfect (and so should others).
- I should always be right.
- Others should behave how I believe they should.
- Life should be fair.
- I shouldn't have to suffer.
- I shouldn't have to endure frustration.
- All of my needs and desires must be satisfied.
- All of my needs and desires should be satisfied if I'm good.
- I should (need to) be able to please everyone all of the time.
- My needs and desires should always take priority over the needs and desires of others.
- I should always know what my needs and desires are at any given time.
- Others should be able to know my needs and desires without my having to tell them.
- If a person loves me, that person should know what I need or desire.
- If a person loves me, that person should always help me get what I believe I need or desire.
- Satisfying one need or desire should make up for not satisfying another need or desire.

The Challenge Regarding Expectations

Deciding whether your expectations are realistic means paying attention to the internal dialogue that tells you how people and life should be versus how they really are. This can be exceedingly challenging. Some have suggested that we should strive to have no expectations since they make us vulnerable to suffering. I counseled a teenager with this attitude, who told himself, "I can't do it, I can't do it, I can't do it," each time he performed a bench press with heavy weights. It was clear that he was protecting himself from disappointment if he failed to reach his goal. But such thoughts only kept him from exerting his full strength to successfully meet the challenge.

Like this young man, you may try to have no expectations in an attempt to avoid pain. When taking this approach, however, you withdraw your emotional investment in life. Embracing life means recognizing your expectations while viewing them as hopes, wishes, or aspirations that can't always be satisfied. And the moment you conclude that you can't satisfy them, you may have to accept that "it is what it is."

Driving Forces: Needs and Desires

At its core, anger derives from the pain of feeling threatened and frustrated that your needs and desires remain unsatisfied. All components in the sequence of anger arousal originate from this point. And yet, anger is a great distraction from looking inward, blinding you to being aware of your needs or desires. Figure 7.8 presents the completed framework for anger.

Your needs and desires serve as the foundation from which your expectations grow. Your needs and desires form a driving force in your life, evolving from your most deeply entrenched values. They serve as the bedrock for your beliefs, emotions, and actions.

Certain needs are embedded in your biology, and their satisfaction is essential for your very survival. These include the need for food, clothing, shelter, and some degree of loving care during your early development.

Much of your life is grounded in needs and desires that are secondary to your needs for survival. These needs and desires are rooted in your personality, and they both influence and are influenced by your emotions, thoughts, and behaviors. Review the following list, here and on the next page, to identify the core forces that most likely drive you:

to feel respected	to feel safe and secure
to feel accepted	to be validated

to feel protected

to satisfy nutritional needs

to feel loved (and to love)

to experience interpersonal connection

to be independent

to be creative

to thrive

to experience control

to feel powerful

to feel optimistic

to feel calm

to feel competent

to be the center of attention

to feel important

to be challenged

to experience self-acceptance

to experience mastery

to experience structure

to experience intimacy

to experience stability

to experience novelty

to be compassionate

to avoid certain feelings

to feel recognized

to experience stability

to experience solitude

Fig. 7.8

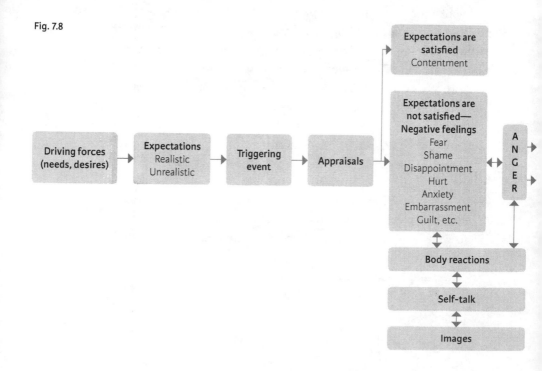

Core Driving Forces and What We Most Value

These core driving forces influence our attitudes and the choices we make every day regarding our friendships, work, leisure time, morality, and worldview. They dictate the priorities in our lives.

For example, some people's intense need for security drives them to compulsively focus on the future. Some may feel a strong desire for novelty, seeking opportunities to explore new places, learn new skills, and meet different people.

Some people's most powerful driving force may be defined by what they strive to avoid rather than by what they seek. For example, the desire to elude feelings of inadequacy or shame often leads to an intense need to be perfect or always right. It's ultimately driven by a desire for internal harmony.

Shifting Priorities

How we prioritize our needs and desires may change over our lifetime. We may have stronger dependency needs as children than as adults. These changing priorities in what we value may compel us to change our lives— whether our relationships, our careers, where we live, or how we spend our leisure time.

Our driving forces may vary from moment to moment. By noon, our need for lunch may take precedence over our need to complete a task we've been working on for several hours. Our desires may shift as the day winds down and we seek quiet time, play, and/or some social activity. And then, at some point in the evening, the need for sleep becomes a priority.

You may find yourself motivated by several driving forces simultaneously. Your desire to be in control may support your need to feel secure. Your desire for acceptance may run parallel with your desire for love and connection. Or, you may find yourself looking for a career that satisfies both your need for financial security and your desire to be creative.

Shifting motivations can affect us daily and in a variety of ways. One of my clients, Wayne, described an interaction with his wife and young daughter that shows this. He had thoroughly enjoyed a Sunday visit with his in-laws, experiencing the joy that comes from spending time with loved ones. During the visit, he was relaxed, attentive, and caring toward his wife and daughter. His behavior immediately changed, however, the moment he started the car to go home. Suddenly, he became irritable and distant. He shared the following with me:

> Only later did I realize it. I became tense as soon as I entered the car. I was so focused on my work. I really wasn't paying attention to my wife or my daughter. I usually keep Sunday free, but this weekend I wasn't able to. I kept putting off working on a report until Sunday evening. I guess I was anxious about what I had to do as well as resentful that I had to do it on the weekend. My main resentment was with work, but I think I took it out on my family.

Wayne remembered the project he had to complete at the very moment he changed his car from park to drive. Within moments, he became a surly and withdrawn husband and father who was less attentive to the needs of his family. This is just one example of how a sudden change in priorities may lead to both anger and anxiety.

Competing Motivating Forces

At times, our motivating forces compete with each other. We may want to share time with our partner but also crave solitude. We may value being creative and want to earn a good income but work in a position that meets our needs only for financial stability. Or, our desire to be creative may compete with our desire for approval.

Competing motivations can lead to moments of tension and irritability, producing the negative feelings that arouse anger. When this occurs, you may direct your low-level anger at the situation, toward others, or toward yourself.

James, twenty-eight years old, longed to become an entrepreneur. He wanted increased control and freedom in his work life. But, when he thought about leaving his company, his need for security often led to anxiety and frustration. Without his full awareness, this conflict caused him to experience ongoing irritability and anger at work and in his relationships. James told me the following:

> I found myself getting irritated over the slightest things at work. Sometimes it was with my supervisor. Sometimes I felt my coworker wasn't up to par in doing her job. I gradually realized I just didn't want to be there. In fact, I had always wanted to be a chef. But after

researching that possibility, I realized I didn't want to work the hours required to be one. I just don't know what I want to do. But I know I'm irritable a lot. I try to keep it to myself. But I know that being snippy or sarcastic at times is my way of dealing with my anger.

Competing motivations are often at the root of the major conflicts we experience in our closest relationships. You may deeply love your partner. At the same time, you may resent your partner if you focus on satisfying his or her needs so much that you fail to satisfy your own. Certainly, a loving relationship means compromise and a desire to please your loved one. Routinely deferring to the needs of a partner, however, can lead to feelings of isolation or powerlessness, potentially causing anger in a relationship.

Core Motivating Forces and Compassion-Focused Theory

In reviewing the list of driving forces, it becomes clear that each reflects a motivation identified by compassion-focused theory: feeling a sense of safety, feeling connection and attachment, and achieving a fulfilling life. Being mindful and self-compassionate about these drives forms the core of healthy anger. And by exploring the meaning of our anger, we connect with our true selves. We become more aware of what we value most.

Such mindfulness offers us more choices. It can motivate us to take the steps that will be the most constructive to satisfying our desires.

* * *

This chapter has focused on a framework that explains the sequence of your anger arousal. It's intended to help you expand your mindfulness about the details of such arousal in your mind and body. As shown in the next chapter, with practice, this model will help you see how your thoughts, feelings, and body interact during anger arousal.

For Further Reflection

1. How did you react to exploring your anger with this format? Try to identify what bodily reactions, if any, you experienced. Did you experience any tension? If so, in what part of your body? You may not recall feeling tension but may still have experienced some as a result of this task.

a. Can you recall the self-talk associated with completing the sequence? Were you critical of the model itself? Did you find yourself experiencing an internal dialogue that reflected the challenges to self-compassion discussed in chapter 2?

b. What emotions did you experience while completing the model in this chapter? Did you experience frustration or annoyance with yourself as a result of difficulty in identifying your reactions?

2. Are you aware of any expectations you may have had about me while you were reading this chapter? How does this framework match up with expectations you may have had regarding how to understand anger?

3. Think of people you interact with throughout the day and try to identify your expectations of them. Then ask yourself how realistic your expectations are.

4. Review the list of appraisals in this chapter and identify those that you often form that may contribute to your anger.

5. Review the list of expectations in this chapter and identify those that you often have that can make you vulnerable to anger.

6. Review the list of driving/core forces in this chapter. Identify those that you believe you value most.

7. What were the driving forces in your anger-arousing situation?

CHAPTER 8

A Tool for Exploring Anger Arousal

In this chapter, you'll find a tool to help expand your mindfulness about your experiences in the framework of anger. The Anger Log is intended to help you understand a current episode of anger and practice healthy anger in the future. Each time you complete the log, you'll become more mindful of your needs and desires as well as the expectations, appraisals, bodily reactions, and negative feelings surrounding your anger.

The Anger Log

The Anger Log will help you examine the chain of internal experiences you've had with anger. This will make you more skillful at altering the course of your anger arousal.

By repeatedly completing the log for different anger episodes, you'll see the patterns in your reactions. You'll also become aware of your hot buttons.

It requires a deep level of awareness to recognize the moment-by-moment experiences that move you to anger. In effect, the log lets you brainstorm alternative ways of reacting to your anger. By reviewing your thoughts and being open to new ways of thinking, you'll assertively practice mindfulness and self-compassion. After some practice, you may be able to observe and identify some of the Anger Log's components in real time. Only continued practice, however, will make you increasingly aware of the complexity of your reactions as they occur. Figure 8.1 shows a blank Anger Log.

Figure 8.1. Anger Log

Motivating forces	→	Expectations	→	Triggering event	→	Appraisals	→	Negative feelings	→	Anger intensity (on a scale of 1 to 10)

Bodily reactions:

Self-talk:

Images:

Previous events and mood prior to triggering event:

You may find completing this log somewhat daunting at first. This makes perfect sense. In part, your anger works to distract you from the discomfort that causes it. As mentioned in chapter 2, you may avoid becoming mindful of your thoughts and feelings due to the distress such self-reflection arouses.

When we pause to reflect on our thoughts, we recognize that some embarrass us and some make absolutely no sense. We have silly thoughts, fearful thoughts, and others that seem shameful. And we have memories we don't want to remember and pain from dreams that remain unfulfilled.

You may find that just thinking about the framework of anger will help you become less reactive, even without completing the Anger Log. The slightest evidence of progress may lead you to conclude that you've mastered your anger. You may do this simply by recognizing and adjusting your unrealistic expectations. Or, you may decide to practice the mindfulness breathing or muscle relaxation techniques described in this book to calm yourself and think before you act.

Your new skills may allow you to successfully derail your anger without having to engage in further self-reflection. Positive changes indicate progress toward healthy anger. But if you don't take the time to complete the

Anger Log, you'll fail to be more fully mindful of the interplay of your needs and desires and the thoughts and feelings that underlie your anger. Practicing healthy anger means not only changing your behaviors in response to anger but also developing new attitudes toward it.

Guidelines for Completing the Anger Log

1. *Calm your mind and body before completing the log.* Complete this log after you've calmed following an episode of anger. This may take hours or even days after the triggering event. The goal, with practice, is for you to be able to analyze your experiences and recognize key elements as they happen in real time.

2. *Become more mindful of your internal experience.* Practice mindfulness breathing for several minutes immediately before completing the log. Evoke your compassionate self to increase your capacity for self-reflection. Mindfulness and self-compassion make you feel safe and fully present with your experience.

3. *Recall the details of the event.* Review a triggering event, as described in chapter 7, by envisioning it as a video recording. Note the details of your surroundings, the person(s) involved, and your internal experiences. Observe the thoughts, feelings, or bodily reactions you experienced. Recall the sights, sounds, and even the temperature of the setting in order to relive what you experienced.

4. *Describe the triggering event.* Complete a brief statement that best defines the triggering event. Use the one that's most relevant to your anger arousal, even if it's a "last straw" incident.

5. *Note your prior history and mood.* Briefly describe situations that may have influenced your mood immediately before the triggering event. This may include triggering events that only annoyed you but contributed to your mind-body state when facing this most recent event.

6. *Rate the intensity of your anger.* Record a rating that reflects the intensity of your anger immediately after the triggering event: 1 indicates the lowest and 10 the most intense.

7. *Identify bodily reactions.* Perform a full body scan from your head to your feet while reviewing your "video" (see chapter 7). This will heighten your mindfulness so that you'll recognize the physical

reactions that occur when you're in the throes of anger. Reviewing the physical reactions described in the next chapter will help you with this.

8. *Identify self-talk.* Record the thoughts that coincided with your negative feelings, including anger. These aren't the appraisals you made immediately after the triggering event but the internal dialogue that followed them.

9. *Identify images.* Briefly describe any images you pictured while you experienced the negative feelings, including anger.

10. *Identify negative feelings.* Identify the negative feelings you experienced immediately before anger arousal. Afterward, review the Feelings List on the facing page to clearly label a feeling you may have experienced but can't identify. This list is invaluable for developing an increased connection with yourself. Skills described in chapter 9 will further help you label these feelings.

11. *Identify the appraisals.* You may initially recognize only one knee-jerk appraisal. With continued practice, you'll usually be able to identify several appraisals that you formed during the event.

12. *Identify the expectations.* First, list those you readily identify. Then review your appraisals. By reviewing the appraisals you formed during the event, you'll more readily recognize expectations you may have had before the triggering event. Be especially mindful to include those that you realize (primarily through hindsight) are illogical or influenced by your child logic. Be alert to any hesitancy to write them down. This will show you how irrational some of your expectations may be. Yes, it's sometimes embarrassing to see how our minds work. Be easy on yourself. This is where your self-compassion will help you have better access to such experiences. Also, be alert to having multiple expectations.

13. *Identify your motivating or driving forces.* What desires or needs did you feel the triggering event was threatening? Review the list of driving forces in chapter 7 to aid you in this process.

Feelings List

abused	delighted	frustrated	powerful
agitated	depleted	furious	powerless
alarmed	depressed	glad	provoked
aloof	despairing	good	regretful
amazed	devalued	grieving	remorseful
angry	diminished	guilty	sad
anguished	disappointed	happy	self-doubting
annoyed	discounted	hate-filled	shocked
anxious	disgusted	helpless	sorrowful
apprehensive	disillusioned	hopeful	surprised
ashamed	desirous	hopeless	tense
awed	disrespected	humiliated	terrorized
betrayed	distrustful	ignored	threatened
bitter	dread-filled	impatient	thrilled
bored	embarrassed	inadequate	unhappy
calm	enraged	irritated	unworthy
cheated	enthusiastic	isolated	vulnerable
cheerful	excitable	jealous	warm
cold	exhilarated	leery	weak
compassionate	exploited	loved	worried
concerned	fearful	mad	worthless
contented	fond	pleased	

How the Anger Log Can Be Useful: Four Vignettes

The rest of this chapter offers four vignettes. Each describes an anger-arousing situation and the Anger Log(s) completed by the individual experiencing it.

Ted: A Girlfriend's Threat to Leave

Ted sought help from me in an effort to keep his girlfriend, Maya. The couple found themselves embroiled in heated arguments within a year after they started dating. Typically, after their exchanges, Maya routinely became quiet and refused to discuss the issue. The last time it happened, she declared, "I'm just going to end this right now!" It was the major triggering event for Ted's anger. During previous arguments, he'd often yelled and cursed. This time, he smashed a lamp on the floor. He told me, and Maya confirmed, that he didn't direct it at her. He provided this explanation:

> I just got so mad! I knew our relationship was on shaky ground because of my anger. I just couldn't hear that she wanted to end it. I just couldn't control myself. I had no intention of hurting her. I felt I just needed to break something. Right after that, for just a moment, I felt a little better. But shortly afterward I knew I was only making it worse.

In hindsight, Ted clearly realized that breaking the lamp released the tension caused by his angry and negative feelings. And he also saw how this anger only fueled Maya's frustrations and her desire to end the relationship. Ted's initial responses on the log are shown in table 8.1.

Ted was aware of his sensitivity to abandonment. He previously had two long-term relationships, both of which his girlfriends had ended. His parents divorced when he was eight, and he spent little time with his father afterward. By further exploring his experience and practicing with the log, Ted identified more of his reactions to the triggering event. These are shown in the more complete log (table 8.2).

Ted had already experienced some fear of abandonment during previous arguments with Maya. Her refusal to talk anymore when things got heated made the problem worse. Ted felt sad, betrayed, powerless, and

Table 8.1. Ted's First Responses on the Anger Log

Motivating forces	→	Expectations	→	Triggering event	→	Appraisals	→	Negative feelings	Anger intensity (on a scale of 1 to 10)
The need for connection, love		We're a couple.		Maya threatening to leave me.		I'll lose her.		Anxious Threatened Frustrated Disrespected	10

Bodily reactions: Intense agitation throughout the body

Self-talk: Not aware of any

Images: None

Previous events and mood prior to triggering event: Prior experiences of fears of abandonment with Maya and prior experiences of fears of abandonment with significant others in early years

Table 8.2. Ted's Second Responses on the Anger Log

Motivating forces	→	Expectations	→	Triggering event	→	Appraisals	→	Negative feelings	→	Anger intensity (on a scale of 1 to 10)
The need for connection, love, control, stability, security		We're a couple.		Maya threatening to leave me.		I'll lose her. It's happening again. She no longer loves me. I'll be alone.		Anxious Threatened Frustrated Disrespected Sad Betrayed Powerless Abandoned		10

Bodily reactions: Intense agitation throughout the body

Self-talk: Not aware of any

Images: None

Previous events and mood prior to triggering event: Prior experiences of fears of abandonment with Maya and prior experiences of fears of abandonment with significant others in early years

abandoned—all of those emotions that accompanied his lonely feelings in the past. His intense anger distracted him from experiencing this pain. Unfortunately, it also kept him from noticing that his anger made Maya feel threatened. Both Ted and Maya focused on their anger instead of their shared hurts and fears.

Betsy: A Friend's Disclosure of a Secret

Betsy experienced a triggering event discussed previously: a friend disclosing a secret that she'd promised not to share. Betsy had started dating Marco shortly after they met at work. She thought she could hide their relationship because they worked in different departments at their firm. And she'd decided to be discreet about their relationship until she was sure what direction it might take. After dating for only two weeks, however, she was unable to contain her excitement. Betsy revealed her secret to Sandra, a coworker with whom she'd developed a good friendship. Betsy fully believed that Sandra could be trusted to keep her promise not to tell anyone.

Understandably, she was surprised and upset when, almost two weeks later, another coworker inquired about how she and Marco were getting along. The coworker confessed that Sandra had revealed Betsy's secret. Betsy became enraged:

> I was furious! I mean, I really thought I could trust Sandra. I know for sure I even told her not to tell anyone. That's what makes me so mad. I immediately called her and without giving her a moment to explain, told her I never wanted to speak to her again. I mean, why would I want to keep her as a friend after that?

This was just one of several experiences with anger that Betsy described. After dating Marco for only two months, she had already lost her temper with him several times. In fact, Betsy sought help only after admitting to herself that her anger had ended her past relationships.

After talking about Sandra, Betsy reported her anger to be a 10 out of 10. When I asked what other emotions she'd felt before becoming angry, Betsy was so intensely angry that she could only name *rage* and *furious* at first. By reviewing the Feelings List, she identified other negative feelings, which are in the completed log (table 8.3).

This vignette demonstrates what often happens when a person first completes the log. You may have difficulty naming feelings other than various

Table 8.3. Betsy's Responses on the Anger Log

Motivating forces →	Expectations →	Triggering event →	Appraisals →	Negative feelings →	Anger intensity (on a scale of 1 to 10)
Desire for honesty	My friend should keep a secret. I should be able to trust a friend.	She revealed my secret.	I can't trust her. I can't trust anyone. I can't maintain my friendship with her.	Betrayed Disappointed Sad Distrustful Disrespected Ignored Discounted	10

Bodily reactions: Tension in chest; increased rate of breathing

Self-talk: I can't believe she did that. I'll get even with her. I specifically told her not to share what I said. (All repeated many times.)

Images: I envisioned Sandra sharing the secret and the other person reacting to it.

Previous events and mood prior to triggering event: Past and recent history of experiences of feeling betrayed and loss of trust forms of anger. With increased mindfulness, you'll be able to identify one or two negative feelings that preceded your anger. Finally, reviewing the Feelings List will show you the variety of emotions that led to your anger.

Certainly, it's natural to feel a range of negative emotions when someone we're close to breaks our trust. Betsy's long history of feeling betrayed, however, fueled her rage. On numerous occasions when younger, Betsy had confided in others only to find her trust broken. By completing the log, Betsy became more aware of this issue.

Betsy's knee-jerk appraisal to end the friendship with Sandra reflected the way Betsy had handled conflicts with her sister in the past: she'd stop speaking to her for months at a time. Similarly, when younger, she quickly ended relationships when hurt or disappointed. Betsy wasn't emotionally prepared to deal with Sandra any other way. She was unable to sit with her feelings and discuss her hurt and disappointment. By examining several anger-arousing situations regarding Marco, Betsy came to better understand her intense reactions.

Jeremy: A Traffic Accident

A court judge referred Jeremy for anger management after Jeremy's violent encounter with another driver on the road. Jeremy readily admitted that he'd had anger issues for some time. Prior to this incident, however, his anger had never led to an involvement with the law.

When stopping at a red light on the way home from work, Jeremy accidentally rear-ended the car in front of him. He described his response as follows:

> The driver of the other car stepped out of his car. He said it was my fault. I couldn't believe it! He caused me to abruptly stop. Sure, I became defensive. I blamed him for the accident. Then he called me "ignorant." That was it! I was furious. My anger went from 0 to 60 in a matter of seconds. I looked around on the ground for something to throw. I picked up a stone and smashed his windshield with it.

Jeremy confessed that it had been many years since he'd been involved in a physical fight. Recently, he'd directed his anger at objects. Fortunately for both drivers, a police officer nearby intervened before the conflict escalated. Jeremy's first anger log is shown in table 8.4.

Table 8.4. Jeremy's First Responses on the Anger Log

Motivating forces		Expectations		Triggering event		Appraisals		Negative feelings		Anger intensity (on a scale of 1 to 10)
Desire for respect; desire to feel in control	→	He should be respectful. He should acknowledge responsibility.	→	Being called "ignorant"	→	He's putting me down. He's not respecting me. He's blaming me. It's not my fault.	→	Devalued Disrespected Criticized	→	10

Bodily reactions: Tension in shoulders and arms; rapid breathing

Self-talk: I can't believe he's saying this. It's his fault.

Images: None

Previous events and mood prior to triggering event: Argument with coworker; past history, in general, specifically related to self-doubt, especially with regard to intelligence

I asked Jeremy whether he thought he'd contributed in any way to the accident. He quickly said, "Not really." Seconds later, however, he sheepishly admitted that he'd been preoccupied with thinking about a coworker he'd quarreled with earlier. I encouraged him to be mindful of his appraisals. By doing this, he was able to provide more details about his experience of anger arousal (table 8.5).

Jeremy recalled that just after the accident, he'd believed he was partially to blame and felt ignorant at not being more careful. Besides feeling devalued by the other driver, Jeremy grew extremely uncomfortable with his feelings of self-doubt, embarrassment, and inadequacy. While completing his log, Jeremy realized that this reaction had stemmed not only from the triggering event of being called ignorant but also from the negative feelings left over from his conflict with his coworker. Jeremy was highly sensitive to criticism, having had long-term doubts about his intelligence. This hot-button sensitivity contributed to his intense reaction.

Wendy: Conflict with a Teenage Daughter

Wendy, a mother of three children, sought my help with conflicts she'd experienced with her older daughter, Heather. They had previously enjoyed a very positive relationship. The tension escalated as Heather reached her

Table 8.5. Jeremy's Second Responses on the Anger Log

Motivating forces	→	Expectations	→	Triggering event	→	Appraisals	→	Negative feelings	→	Anger intensity (on a scale of 1 to 10)
Desire for respect; desire to feel in control; desire to see self as bright, loved, confident		He should be respectful. He should acknowledge responsibility.		Being called "ignorant"		He's putting me down. He's not respecting me. He's blaming me. It's not my fault.		Devalued Disrespected Criticized		10
						It is my fault. I should have been more careful. I am ignorant.		Embarrassed Disappointed with self Self-doubting Inadequate		

Bodily reactions: Tension in shoulders and arms; rapid breathing

Self-talk: I can't believe he's saying this. It's his fault.

Images: None

Previous events and mood prior to triggering event: Argument with coworker plus past history of self-doubt, especially with regard to intelligence

early teens. Wendy reported having few problems with her younger daughter and son.

Wendy described numerous occasions over the previous months when she'd gotten angry at Heather. I suggested she explore her experiences surrounding any one interaction. She described the following exchange:

> We argued recently when Heather asked to stay over at a friend's house on Saturday night. I'd already planned a family visit with my parents for that night. Lately, we don't get to see them that often. So I wanted the whole family to be together. I immediately got angry and told her she was being selfish. She yelled, saying I was controlling and possessive. She immediately stormed off to her room. She eventually came with us but she was quiet and withdrawn the whole evening. Lately, we just keep arguing with each other.

Wendy completed a log regarding this event (table 8.6). This first log seems to show a typical parent-teenager relationship. But when Wendy took a closer look at their clashes, they clearly weren't caused by the normal strains of adolescent angst. Wendy told me she'd felt increasingly isolated in her relationship with her husband, Roger:

> Up until about five years ago, Roger and I were very close—emotionally and physically. During this time, we've become much more distant and tense with each other. Roger lost his job four years ago and was unemployed for six months. That led to a big decrease in his income. He really changed after that. Then I gradually gained weight and, to be honest, I wasn't feeling good about myself. I certainly felt like I was less desirable, anyway.

Wendy said that she deeply loved her children. She had no regrets about putting her career on hold to be a full-time stay-at-home mom. She soon realized, however, that Heather's move toward independence stirred Wendy's own fears about the future and being alone. Although she had two younger children, these encounters with Heather brought a variety of feelings to the surface. She realized that because she felt so lonely in her marriage, she depended on Heather for emotional closeness. I encouraged her to look at her other reactions to the triggering event, and Wendy filled out a second log (table 8.7).

Table 8.6. Wendy's First Responses on the Anger Log

Motivating forces	→	Expectations	→	Triggering event	→	Appraisals	→	Negative feelings	Anger intensity (on a scale of 1 to 10)
To be respected		She should listen to me.		She's challenging me.		She's being defiant and disrespectful.		Ignored	8
								Disrespected	
						She's being stubborn.		Frustrated	
								Sad	

Bodily reactions: Tension in the face

Self-talk: I will not let her go.

Images: Showing up at parents' house without her

Previous events and mood prior to triggering event: Past conflicts with Heather and sensitivities regarding control in earlier relationships

Table 8.7. Wendy's Second Responses on the Anger Log

Motivating forces	→	Expectations	→	Triggering event	→	Appraisals	→	Negative feelings	→	Anger intensity (on a scale of 1 to 10)
Desire for closeness, meaning		She should listen to me. Our closeness should never change.		She's challenging me.		She's being defiant and disrespectful. She's being stubborn. I'm losing her.		Ignored Disrespected Frustrated Sad Anxious Abandoned		8

Bodily reactions: Tension in the face

Self-talk: I will not let her go.

Images: Showing up at parents' house without her

Previous events and mood prior to triggering event: Past conflicts with Heather and sensitivities regarding control in past relationships

Although Wendy had been somewhat absorbed by her own insecurities, she wasn't so self-absorbed that she couldn't see how her fear of losing her husband negatively affected her daughter.

* * *

All of these clients worked on their mindfulness and self-compassion skills in order to better understand their complex anger issues. They also became more self-aware of how their habits of thinking, feeling, and behaving influenced their quickness to anger. The remaining chapters offer practices to help you explore your own habits in greater detail on your path to healthy anger.

For Further Reflection

1. Which components of the Anger Log did you find the hardest to identify?

2. Were you aware of any self-talk you experienced while reading any part of this chapter? If so, do you believe that you experienced tension related to any of the challenges identified in chapter 2?

3. At this moment, how strong is your motivation to cultivate healthy anger? How can you further your commitment?

4. I strongly encourage you to review your answers to question 4 in the For Further Reflection section of chapter 2. As I'll keep emphasizing, reminding yourself why you're reading this book will help you to be mindful and patient with yourself while working to practice healthy anger.

CHAPTER 9

Mindfulness and Self-Compassion for Your Feelings

Being aware of your emotions is essential for survival. It helps you detect threats from within your body as well as those from your environment. Beyond survival, such self-awareness helps you identify your likes, dislikes, needs, and desires. It supports your understanding of and compassion toward yourself and others. It also supports your goals in life, including the development of meaningful relationships.

Practicing healthy anger calls for skills that include awareness, differentiation, and the ability to effectively manage your feelings. These skills have been associated with improved psychological well-being, health, relationships, and employability.[1] This chapter offers exercises to help you become more mindful of and compassionate toward your feelings. These strategies play a significant role in overcoming destructive anger.

Emotional Awareness

Your ability to be emotionally aware rests on mindfully acknowledging and accepting your feelings—and distinguishing among them. This awareness means being open to observing your emotions rather than "overreacting and amplifying what you perceive . . . it is a natural mode that maintains self-reflectiveness even amidst turbulent emotions."[2] Such mindfulness lets you realize that you don't have to act on or eliminate your feelings.

Encouragement and modeling may have helped you learn how to play tennis, strum a guitar, or speak another language. Just as detailed feedback is necessary to learn these skills, emotional awareness depends on knowing the details of your emotional experiences. Remember that feelings may range from vague and hard to distinguish to distinct and easily recognizable.

The exercises in this chapter will help you access, recognize, and distinguish your emotions. You'll become more mindful of your internal emotional landscape as a necessary step toward healthy anger.

EXERCISE

Slowing Down

As described in earlier chapters, your emotions are embedded in your body. You just have to listen to them. This requires you to create a certain open state of mind and body. This exercise, based on psychologist Alan Fogel's practices, will slow your attention down and help you achieve this goal.[3]

Sit or lie down in a comfortable place where you won't be disturbed. Focus on mindfulness breathing for a few minutes. At some point, your attention will shift. Notice where it takes you. Perhaps you heard the sound of rain against the window. Maybe your stomach grumbled. Concentrate on just one thought, regardless of where your mind goes. Focusing your attention is a major part of slowing it down.

Repeat this thought to yourself several times. You may find it helpful to say it out loud. Maybe you see images in your mind that go along with the thought. Focus on them for a moment. Repeat this for a while and then observe any sensations or emotions that you feel.

Perhaps other thoughts are coming to you as you do this. Stay with them if they're related to your original thought. Slow down to see whether any sensations or emotions arise. Like the images you form with the visualization techniques you've learned from this book, these may feel fleeting.

This process of unraveling takes time. It's a process of waiting and letting feelings and sensations seep into your awareness. Keep returning to this exercise even when you may experience nothing.

Mindfulness about Emotion in Your Body

This mindfulness exercise offers another way to stay in touch with your emotions. It can be especially useful when you're dealing with a difficult emotion such as anger or one of the feelings that precede anger. I recommend working with one emotion at a time. This exercise is a variation of one described by psychologist Christopher Germer.[4]

Make yourself comfortable in a place where you won't be disturbed. Gently close your eyes and engage in mindfulness meditation for a few minutes. Mindfully scan your body—both its surface and its interior. Notice any sensations. Notice the air moving past your nostrils or the rise and fall of your chest. Do this for several minutes.

Shift your attention from your breathing and think of a negative emotion you wish to address. Recall a situation that aroused this emotion. While doing this, scan your body to observe where you feel tension most strongly. Keep scanning your body for any signs of tension.

Return your attention to the area where you feel the most tension. Continue your relaxed breathing but imagine and feel your breath surrounding and soothing that area. Do this for several moments.

If the feeling gets too uncomfortable, focus again on your breathing. Once you become calmer, concentrate on the emotion again. Finish by practicing your breathing for several minutes and then open your eyes.

Informal Mindful Reflection on Emotions

Mindful reflection offers a powerful way to connect with your feelings. You can practice it as described above or informally throughout the day. For example, if you find yourself feeling vaguely unsettled, take a moment to think about the events or thoughts you experienced in the hours prior to your mood. This can help you determine the cause of your feeling. It requires you to identify and distinguish the emotions associated with feeling unsettled. Be mindful of the fact that your mood could also be tied to thoughts about a *future* event.

Many years ago, I had an experience that shows how this exercise works. On a Friday evening, I'd just entered a lane to my bank's drive-through window to withdraw money. Two cars sat in front of me. As I waited, the person at the window seemed to be taking an excessive amount of time making a transaction. So, I gently sounded my car's horn a few times. (I was much more impatient many years ago.) The driver immediately in front of me turned around to look at me, with a facial expression of annoyance and confusion. I immediately felt embarrassed. The woman who faced me appeared to be in her eighties. I did my best to apologize by mouthing, "I'm sorry!" And then I waited patiently until it was my turn.

About five minutes later, after finishing at the bank, I suddenly felt unsettled. While stopped at a traffic light, I scanned my body. My mood was "down," although I had no idea why. I reviewed thoughts and events in my mind—those that had recently occurred and those regarding the anticipated weekend. I'd experienced a satisfactory day at work. I couldn't identify anything that would prevent me from enjoying my weekend. I pondered the matter while driving several blocks, and then it hit me.

I'd experienced a delayed reaction to the event from just minutes before. Believing that I'd annoyed the elderly driver left me with a range of emotions. I realized that I felt embarrassed, guilty, and maybe even a little ashamed. I had based my entire career on being compassionate and helping people feel better, but my child logic had clearly been activated. I judged myself for what I'd done.

My down mood completely subsided when I realized how it had happened. Afterward, I engaged in a self-compassionate dialogue, which I'll discuss in the next chapter. This helped me sit with my feelings and move past them.

Experiential Avoidance

All too often, people manage their feelings in ways that make those feelings inaccessible. We often wonder why, as adults, we find it difficult to answer the question, "What am I feeling?" It's understandable why we may hesitate or avoid asking this question. And it's not surprising that we may expend great effort fleeing our uncomfortable feelings.

The psychologist Stephen Hayes, a founder of *acceptance and commitment therapy*, refers to this tendency as *experiential avoidance*, the avoidance of "the immediate experience of a negative, private event such as an unwanted thought, feeling, memory, or physical sensation."[5]

Destructive anger is just one way to express such avoidance. It distracts us from experiencing the various negative emotions that may prompt it. To a certain extent, destructive anger is influenced by *suppression* and *repression*.

Suppression and repression both keep us unaware of our feelings. With suppression, we mindfully remove feelings from our awareness by ignoring, forgetting, or minimizing them.[6] And the more uncomfortable we become with such feelings, the more our unconscious mind may try to keep us unaware of them: this process is repression. Mindfulness, self-compassion, and the practices in this chapter can help bring these feelings to the surface.

At times, choosing suppression may be wise. It can be very constructive to suppress acting on your anger until you've made sense of it. Only then will you improve at noting and exploring the feelings and expectations you've experienced during conflicts. This will make you more aware of your most valued needs and desires. Keep in mind, however, that suppression becomes destructive when you shelve your feelings without facing them. Over time, it will usually lead to an increase in discontent and anger.

Experiential Avoidance of Your Anger

You may suffer frequent, intense, long-lasting anger and yet find it so repulsive that you suppress or repress it. This can be challenging. If you take this attitude toward anger, training yourself to become aware of it requires self-compassion. You'll need to evoke your compassionate self rather than use tough love. You must remind yourself that anger is natural and a part of the human condition. It's especially helpful to remember that anger itself is very different from aggressively acting out your anger.

Be Mindful of Judging Your Negative Feelings

When given a choice, most of us prefer not to experience negative feelings. After all, they cause us great discomfort. All too often, however, we suffer not only because we feel such feelings but because we judge ourselves for having them. I've worked with many people who grew depressed or angry about their depression, angry about their anxiety, anxious about their anger, or even angry about their anger. They judged themselves after comparing their true experiences with what they believed their experiences *should have been*. Some people see themselves as weak because they experience certain negative feelings. Others may believe they don't deserve to have them. And some may resent having such feelings, believing that others never have to endure them.

Becoming more mindful of your emotions depends partly on being mindful of how and when you judge them. You'll need to identify the emotions you least want to feel, the emotions that cause you the most shame or embarrassment, and the emotions that cause you the greatest anxiety. Review the Feelings List in chapter 8. Identify the feelings that you find the most uncomfortable. You may be the most judgmental about these feelings. Being mindful of your judgments will help you recognize those feelings that cause your anger—with others and with yourself.

Mixed or Contradictory Emotional Reactions That Include Anger

Healthy emotional awareness includes recognizing and accepting mixed emotions—two or more emotions that occur simultaneously or in sequence. Our subconscious feelings seek expression even when we're not aware of them. This makes sense. These feelings are rooted in underlying needs that seek recognition. When we ignore or minimize them, we may behave in ways that seem confusing, both to others and ourselves.

Alex sought help with anger, at his wife's request. She was concerned about how he disciplined their children. He was never physically aggressive, but he often became loud and threatening.

When questioned about how he was disciplined as a child, Alex initially said, "Oh, my parents? They were always very loving. Oh, sure, my father occasionally yelled at us. And he sometimes hit us with a paddle. But it was always on the bottom. And we usually deserved it. No big deal." Alex described several such occasions, all with a smile. After these disclosures, he always mentioned how much he loved his parents.

In time, Alex came to better understand his feelings. He gradually realized how angry and sad he felt about how he was disciplined as a child. He loved his parents dearly and felt very guilty about his anger. He immediately countered his feelings with recollections of how loving his parents were, the moment he felt this anger. The challenge he faced in recognizing mixed feelings came from several factors.

It's often easier to think globally, in black and white terms. *Global thinking*, as discussed in the next chapter, leads us to ignore the finer details of our emotional experience. Alex isn't alone. Recognizing mixed or ambivalent feelings in our most loving relationships is a major challenge for many of us. Accepting these feelings is yet another aspect of accepting our humanity.

Be Mindful of Distractions

Many people engage in various distractions to cope with or avoid their feelings. Some use alcohol. While alcohol is often a normal part of one's social life, and a glass of wine may enhance the pleasure of a fine meal, even low amounts can quiet the "white noise" of anxiety or other negative emotions.

Smoking cigarettes or marijuana can also provide an escape from uncomfortable feelings. Others lose themselves in work, in exercise, or in eating in an effort to ignore certain emotional experiences.

While it clearly offers a wide range of benefits, the Internet, unfortunately, has become a major distraction for some. Playing video games, reading blogs, or even just surfing can keep someone from dealing with feelings in his or her daily life.

Procrastination is another effective strategy to avoid experiencing negative emotions and thoughts. Mindfully identifying and fully accepting the feelings we encounter when moving forward in a task is the first step to overcoming procrastination.

If you'd like to identify some of the feelings that may distract you, pause when you experience the urge to engage in any of these activities. Take your emotional pulse. Mindfully tune in to your body to discover what feelings are stirring—and whether you're trying to avoid them.

Distinguishing between Thoughts and Feelings

All too often, our quickness to anger may be based on our difficulty distinguishing between our thoughts and our feelings. This process may seem highly puzzling to some. Being able to make this distinction is one of the challenges of trying to access our feelings. The following illustrates a conversation I've had with many people who have struggled with this task.

> Bernie: So, your triggering event was your boss telling you that you were getting a rating of "satisfactory'" on your overall annual evaluation?
>
> Jake: Yeah. I definitely thought I deserved a better rating, especially for how hard I've worked this year.

Bernie: So, on a 1 to 10 scale, how angry did you become in reaction to receiving that evaluation?

Jake: At first it was about 8, but as I continued talking with him and realized he wasn't going to budge, it very quickly went to 10.

Bernie: Now recall that interaction and how you felt just before you experienced anger. Rewind your "video" and observe what you experienced.

Jake: I thought he was being a jerk. Excuse the cursing, but I thought he was a bastard! He was completely unfair.

Bernie: Let me clarify. I asked what feelings you had in reaction to the evaluation and you described your thoughts about him.

Jake: All right. I felt he was being a bastard!

Bernie: That is an observation. How did you feel when you concluded he was being a "bastard"?

Jake: I don't deserve that treatment. I deserve better.

Bernie: How do you feel when you aren't treated in a way that you feel you deserve?

Jake: Well, I was definitely disappointed and frustrated.

Bernie: Pause there for a moment. Those are feelings. They're observations of your inner experience rather than observations of the other person. They show how your boss's behavior affected you internally. Feelings result from observing your mind and body, scanning your internal reactions, and labeling what you find. Here is a list of feelings [handing him the Feelings List shown in chapter 8]. Scan this list to see if you can identify any other feelings you may have experienced immediately before becoming angry—feelings that "pushed" you into anger.

As suggested in chapter 8, I recommend that you first recall your feelings without viewing the list. Afterward, use it to identify any additional feelings that resonate with you.

Ethan, a high school teacher who had been married for three years, faced a similar challenge.

Ethan: I came home from work, and I couldn't believe it. She did it again! This time Dana bought an exercise bike even though we agreed not to until we researched the best buy. And she got the most expensive one we looked at.

Bernie: How did you react?

Ethan: I asked her what she was thinking.

Bernie: Did you tell her how you felt?

Ethan: Oh, I'm sure she knew how I felt. I yelled at her and told her she was being ignorant.

Bernie: Can you recall saying anything else?

Ethan: Yeah. First, I told her that she needs to watch how much she spends this month. We've had unusual expenses, and I didn't want to put more charges on the card.

Bernie: Anything else?

Ethan: I told her I felt that she has no consideration for what I think.

Now, take a moment to identify those feelings that you believe Ethan experienced in reaction to his wife's purchase. Although he described words and a tone of voice reflecting anger, Ethan never actually told his wife that he was angry. Calling her ignorant, telling her what to do, and referring to her as inconsiderate are all thoughts rather than feelings. I probed a little further to help him clarify, especially regarding his feelings immediately before becoming angry.

Bernie: Review this incident on your imaginary video. Picture walking into your home and pausing at the moment you see the bike. What did you feel?

Ethan: Frankly, I was pissed! I was angry right away.

Bernie: So you were angry. Can you identify which negative feelings pushed you into anger?

Ethan: Yeah. I felt like, again she just ignored me . . . And, I know I immediately felt like, again, I can't trust her to keep her word when it comes to money.

Ethan said, "She just ignored me," rather than "I felt ignored." And "I can't trust her," rather than "I felt distrustful." This slight difference demonstrates that Ethan is observing his experience rather than observing his emotions. Even when I inquired further, Ethan found it hard to identify his feelings toward his wife's purchase and instead shared his thoughts. Only after more discussion and a review of the Feelings List did Ethan recognize feeling disappointment, frustration, distrust, being ignored, and a low-level sense of betrayal with regard to his wife not keeping her word. When we focused on his concern over their finances, he quickly realized that seeing the bike made him immediately anxious.

When asked how they feel about someone verbally attacking them, it's not unusual for people to respond: "He's a jerk!" "She's ignorant!" Or, "He just likes to make you mad." All of these responses are examples of thoughts, not feelings. However, people's statements that they felt "attacked," "threatened," or "frustrated" clearly express their feelings and the way the experience affected them.

The following four guidelines can help you distinguish between thoughts and feelings:

1. Identifying how you feel means noting your internal experience and observing *your* emotions or feelings as reflected by your mind-body state.

2. You're most likely stating a thought if you make an observation about someone else when trying to identify your feelings.

3. A simple statement of emotional impact is "I *feel [feeling word]* when . . ." If you replace *feel* with *think* and your statement doesn't make sense, you're observing a feeling. For example, "I feel disappointed" versus "I think disappointed."

4. Feelings are most often described by one word rather than by a phrase or sentence. Simply stated, "When others do _____ I feel _____."

Take Your Emotional Pulse

You can also become more mindful of your feelings by taking your "emotional pulse" several times a day—pausing to pinpoint your feelings at any given moment. Start by observing your feelings the same time each day for a couple of weeks. Then vary the times of day you do this so that you get a wider sampling.

Simply ask yourself, "What am I feeling right now?" Sometimes, you may clearly identify feelings. At other times, your feelings may seem vague, muted, or complex. Review the Feelings List following your first analysis. Rate the intensity of your feelings from 1, a low intensity, to 10, the highest intensity. Be attentive to whether you're experiencing a cluster of feelings rather than a single feeling or emotion. Review your logs at the end of the week to note any patterns. Also, look for patterns in each experience that may arouse specific feelings.

The Intensity and Pervasiveness of Feelings

Another way to connect with our feelings involves being mindful of their strength and how they influence our lives. A feeling may be fleeting, or it may extend over time to become a mood. It may also be a more dominant aspect of one's personality, known as a *trait*. For example, anxiety, pessimism, or even hopefulness may play a major role in your general outlook and predisposition. Finally, some feelings may be strong enough to interfere with your functioning, thus qualifying as a disorder and possibly requiring professional counseling.

Look to the Past

As emphasized throughout this book, events from your past often affect the arousal or intensity of your anger—as well as your difficulty in letting anger go. Such events could be from the recent or the more distant past.

Destructive anger often arises from severe hurts suffered in past close relationships, whether with parents or others. These experiences can leave people with unrealistic expectations about current relationships. Some believe that those with whom they now have relationships should make up for or compensate for the pain they've experienced in the past, but the past is the past.

Many clients I work with are quick to deny the impact of their past, in part because they've never allowed themselves to experience hurt or anger over it. These individuals are often uneasy about seeking help. They can experience great distress as a result of the anger or blame they feel toward their parents or others. At times, their child logic is at work, which may keep them from admitting to such feelings.

Looking to the past is about explaining rather than blaming. It's about recognizing how the past influences our feelings, thoughts, and behaviors. Being mindful and self-compassionate means knowing how both your recent and your distant past influence your anger. Ultimately, chronic anger issues are very much based on unresolved feelings surrounding past suffering. At times, you must explore the anguish from your past to make peace with it and move forward. Looking at our history helps us explore and identify unmet needs, the pain surrounding our attempts to satisfy them, and the anger that may result from both.

Some of the questions in the For Further Reflection section at the end of each chapter offer an opportunity to do this. Chapter 11 shows how to use the Anger Log to expand your awareness to your past and your anger issues. While all of the strategies in this book offer insights and skills to embrace healthy anger, you may decide that counseling would help with this process.

Anger and Its Relationship to Three Other Negative Emotions

Although anger is often a reaction to other negative emotions—accompanied by feeling threatened—it interacts with several key emotions that deserve further attention. Understanding these interactions can give you greater insight into the emotional landscape of your life.

Anger and Anxiety

Some of us become angry in reaction to anxiety. And some of us become anxious about becoming angry. Experiencing some level of anxiety in reaction to anger is a good thing. It can motivate us to change. Lacking anxiety, we may feel less restrained in how we manage anger. Anxiety, like guilt, causes us to think about something before doing it, leading to more constructive decisions and actions.

Some overlap exists in your body's reactions to anxiety and anger, and both result from a feeling of being threatened. Often, anxiety leads you to withdraw while anger moves you to act. Anxiety may be the response when anger threatens your sense of self. Or, anger can be a way of escaping the discomfort of anxiety.

A software designer I worked with formed a business partnership with two of his longtime friends. During the first few years of their association, he grew increasingly angry over what he perceived to be his partners' failures. Anxiety, based on his financial fears, lingered beneath his anger. The partnership activated his hot-button trust issues as well. He frequently viewed their differences of opinion as a sure sign of the business breaking up, creating intense anxiety that he tried to ignore, minimize, or deny. His anger toward his partners masked his deeper anxiety about the company's future.

In a recent study, anger was found to contribute to symptoms in individuals suffering from *generalized anxiety disorder*, characterized by free-floating worry.[7] Anger, like anxiety, is often caused by feeling as if you lack control. Clearly, these two emotions can fuel each other.

Anger and Depression

Your tendency to become depressed depends on both genetic factors and life experiences. Some of the symptoms include a depressed mood, major changes in sleep or appetite, lethargy and fatigue, lack of interest or pleasure in activities, and/or feelings of hopelessness and worthlessness. When we're depressed, we feel isolated and powerless when trying to meet the challenges of life. We believe that negative events are beyond our control. As a result, depression often prevents us from taking positive actions that would help our situation.

Anger is often a reaction to feeling depressed, arising from feelings of pessimism and hopelessness. While both men and women become depressed, men seem to have more difficulty recognizing depression and admitting to it. They often believe such feelings threaten their manliness, and they are more likely to resort to anger to distract themselves from their depression.[8]

Even low-level depression can lead to an increased brittleness in mood and negative emotions in general—especially anger. Depression may also result from dwelling on regrets about past decisions or lost opportunities. These sources of pain can lead to ongoing resentment and even bitterness.

The depression that accompanies illness may also contribute to anger. Illness sometimes involves a loss of function, whether temporary or permanent. The degree of anger may depend on one's expectations. For example, some people expect, unrealistically, that they should be invincible or immune to aging. They may believe illness is unfair. These beliefs may only exacerbate their quickness to anger.

Anger, especially repressed anger, can be a major contributor to depression. Many people suffer from depression because they've failed to acknowledge that their anger stems from deeply rooted past hurts. They may feel guilty and ashamed about their anger, which fuels a weak sense of self-worth. This is a formula for the hopelessness and helplessness that are the hallmarks of intense depression.

Depression may stem from early childhood experiences that include emotional or physical abuse or neglect. We can still suffer from emotional pain, however, even if we had well-meaning and loving parents. Perhaps they behaved hurtfully, and we feared sharing our feelings with them. We may have been afraid to express or even experience anger. We may have believed that our loving parents would never have behaved in such a way unless we did something wrong. These types of experiences can lead us to direct our anger inward.

Studies suggest that we're more likely to experience depression as adults when we've been shamed as children.[9] Shame and depression are very much related. Shame can contribute to depression, and shame can arise when we berate ourselves for experiencing depression. Either situation can leave us prone to anger.

It's understandable that depression can lead to anger and anger can lead to depression. And it's equally understandable that negative attitudes can undermine the practice of self-compassion, which is essential for self-connection, understanding, and self-soothing.

Anger and Shame

Shame and the desire to avoid experiencing it are often the driving forces behind anger. Some researchers suggest that shame comes about from repeatedly being told, not that we did something bad, but that we *are* something bad.[10] Shame, like guilt and embarrassment, involves negatively judging ourselves when we believe we've failed to live up to either our own standards or the standards of other people.[11] Others who study shame view it more as a response when "we think we're moving closer to becoming undesired and undesirable in the eyes of others and in the eyes of ourselves."[12]

Certainly, a little bit of guilt and embarrassment can help keep us socialized. After all, we do need to follow certain norms and expectations of the society we live in. The problem arises when we experience *toxic shame*—shame that paralyzes us in all aspects of life.

Michael Lewis, a psychologist and author, cites three key features that form the experience of shame: (1) the desire to hide; (2) intense pain, discomfort, and anger; and (3) the feeling that one is no good, inadequate, and unworthy.[13] Some words used to express the emotion of shame include feeling *insecure, worthless, stupid, foolish, silly,* and so on.[14] Shame can foster an overriding sense of self-disgust that, when extreme, can even lead to self-loathing. At such moments, we feel completely worthless rather than realizing that everyone fails in some aspect of their lives.

Feelings of shame lead to the belief that we don't belong in our communities or the larger part of humanity. Shame can cause us to withdraw and turn inward. It ultimately leads to our feeling isolated. It also keeps us from being self-compassionate and shuts the door to our accepting compassion from others. Shame and guilt both arise from negative self-evaluation. Shame is more general, whereas guilt often focuses on a particular action. Guilt also drives us to do our best to alter a situation.

The quickness to feel shame is often rooted in our childhood. Experiences that foster a negative image of ourselves can make us prone to shame. Children and teens who blame themselves for being abused or neglected or for their family's emotional difficulties may tend to experience shame. Children and teens who practice tough love on themselves are more likely to feel shame than others.

Language that reflects global and critical evaluations of who we are makes us especially vulnerable to shame. The following anecdote illustrates this.

Suppose that, as a four-year-old child, you spilled your milk on the kitchen table. A compassionate parent would say something along the lines of: "It was an accident. We all have accidents. I'll help you. Let's clean it up together. Next time, just pay a little more attention." This response emphasizes our shared humanity in our capacity to have accidents. It focuses on the action of having spilled milk rather than on you as a person. Your parent offers to help you address the incident, demonstrating that the world and loved ones can be supportive. Finally, your parent provides feedback by suggesting you be more attentive the next time. This guidance can help you become more responsible and avoid such accidents in the future.

In contrast, perhaps one of the most powerfully shame-inducing responses your parent could offer would be something like: "You're so clumsy! You're so stupid! You do that all the time. You never pay attention to what you do. Look at the mess you made!" Clearly, this is an evaluation of the whole you—one that's shaming. It's conveyed in anger and communicates disappointment and disgust. It's global rather than specifically focused on one aspect of your behavior. It's global in using such terms as *clumsy, stupid, all the time*, and *never*. It shows no compassion and fosters attitudes that undermine the development of self-compassion. And finally, it offers no constructive feedback about how to avoid such events in the future.

When frequent and pervasive, such responses from your parent might dictate how you manage criticism and feedback in general. Suppose we flash-forward several years. You're in the second grade and have just turned in a writing assignment to your teacher. The teacher says you did a good job but that one word seems out of place. You'd most likely be receptive to the teacher's comments if your important caretakers, including past teachers, had given you compassionate feedback focused on specific actions. You'd objectively consider the feedback without spiraling into shame and anger. You would be more realistic and self-compassionate as you acknowledged that learning means sometimes making mistakes.

Instead, suppose you've developed a tendency to experience shame. You'd be quick to view the feedback as simply another global and negative evaluation of you as a person. You'd completely ignore the warm tone of the teacher's voice, the fact that you made only a small mistake, or even the compliment the teacher paid you on your writing as a whole. You'd become angry. In response, you might rip up the paper and once again conclude that you hate teachers, school, and perhaps authority in general.

Our tendency to experience shame strongly influences all of our relationships and how we respond to life's challenges. And our quickness to anger can effectively help us escape from shame's powerful grip. Jean, one of my clients, illustrates how shame can affect anger arousal.

Jean was a college student in her twenties who suffered from a lack of motivation and low-level depression. Her tendency to be a perfectionist and her quickness to criticize herself paralyzed her in her classes. She confessed that she would never ask a question for fear of appearing ignorant. Several sessions later, she described recalling an early childhood experience like others I've been told about numerous times over the years.

She recalled her mother teaching her to swim. At first, they stood together in the shallow end of the pool. Suddenly, without any warning, her mother picked her up and threw her into the deep end.

I immediately reacted with sadness as I asked what she recalled about the experience. Jean said that she tried her best to swim. But because she became overwhelmed with panic, she merely thrashed about and swallowed too much water to continue. She believed that she should have been able to swim. And she remembered being highly disappointed and angry with herself for failing at it.

I suggested that she might have learned a lesson from her experience with her mother, but that it wasn't about swimming. I suggested that she might have taken to heart the guideline "I should know what I don't know." Jean soon realized how the shame she'd felt because of this unrealistic expectation led to difficulties in many areas of her life.

I've worked with many men who experienced similar shameful feelings as children. As adults, these men direct their anger outward. They often need to be right or perfect. In an effort to escape feeling shame, they're intent on proving others wrong. Being argumentative and overbearing are just two ways they manage this internal conflict. Rather than recognize and accept their self-doubt or shame, they may even use anger so that others will concede or back away from the discussion.

Shame is perhaps the most powerful barrier to self-compassion. And cultivating self-compassion has been associated with a decrease in shame, anxiety, depression, self-criticism, inferiority, and submissive behavior and an increase in the ability to be self-soothing and self-reassuring.[15]

* * *

Becoming mindful of thoughts that may promote or reflect shame is a major challenge to cultivating compassion. The chapter that follows helps you to meet this challenge.

For Further Reflection

1. Identify and put into words, as clearly as possible, the guidelines you've been practicing and telling yourself regarding shame, depression, anger, and anxiety.

2. To what degree do you believe that shame and trying to avoid shame contribute to your anger? For example:

    a. How often do you become angry with yourself for failing to measure up to your own expectations?

    b. How often do you become angry when criticized?

3. Be mindful of how self-doubt may also contribute to shame.

4. If you experience shame, is it mostly related to specific areas or general?

5. Do you experience anxiety after you get angry? If so, how might this be helpful for you?

CHAPTER 10

Mindfulness and Self-Compassion for Your Thoughts

Practicing mindfulness and self-compassion toward your thoughts frees you to accept them as just part of a variety of thoughts you could be thinking. Such mindfulness can help you distinguish whether certain thoughts stem from your emotions or from your rational mind. The skill to make this distinction provides a meaningful moment of choice. It can help you think more clearly, which is essential to controlling your anger. It will also make you more flexible in your thinking and, as a result, less vulnerable to feeling threatened and reacting to potentially triggering events. Furthermore, being aware of your thoughts helps you to better identify your needs and desires and distinguish between them.

You must evoke your compassionate self to be truly open to your thoughts. Compassion is especially important because discovering how you think can both surprise and threaten you. This insight can sway your motivation to stay committed to the practice of self-compassion and healthy anger.

Mindfulness about Your Appraisals

The following strategies can help you clearly recognize the knee-jerk appraisals that you form for triggering events. Specifically, they'll help you become mindful of the patterns of thinking that lead to such thoughts.

Self-Inquiry about Your Appraisals

Repeatedly completing the Anger Log will help you to more accurately identify the appraisals you form in response to triggering events. Some appraisals may be easy to identify. Others require deeper self-reflection. The following dialogue can be used as a model for reflecting on and inquiring about your own experience.

> Charles: Matt, my six-year-old, got really upset the other night. I had told him to put his toys away and get ready for bed. But he just continued to play with them. He completely disrespected me. I got angry and yelled at him. I told him he had just three more minutes. I left the room and when I returned, his toys were still scattered on the floor. I immediately grabbed the toys out of his hand and threw them in the toy box. He started to cry and have a tantrum. At that point, I scooted him out of the living room and into the bathroom to brush his teeth. So, the triggering event was his not getting ready for bed.
>
> Bernie: And your appraisals?
>
> Charles: He just wasn't doing what he was told to do.
>
> Bernie: Any others?
>
> Charles: Oh, yeah. He wasn't respecting me.
>
> Bernie: Any others?
>
> Charles: Well, I don't know. This was the third time this week that this has happened.
>
> Bernie: Did you think that he was doing it purposely to annoy you?
>
> Charles: No, I think I've made progress there.
>
> Bernie: Do you mean that you made that appraisal in the past, but you caught yourself this time from buying into it?
>
> Charles: Yeah . . . but, as I think about it, I guess one of my appraisals was "It's happening again!"
>
> Bernie: And if that was one of your appraisals, your reactions are not just to this single triggering event.
>
> Charles: Oh, definitely. I very quickly thought about the last time he did the same thing. It was just two nights before.
>
> Bernie: How much time did it take you the last time to get him to bed?
>
> Charles: Actually, it took me about twenty minutes to get him calmed down.

Bernie: Do you think one of your appraisals was "Again, I'm going to have to spend twenty minutes getting him to sleep"?

Charles: Yes. I immediately thought that this would be a repeat of the other night. In fact, thinking about it now, I think I actually said, "Not again!" out loud.

Bernie: What else was going on while you were having this interaction with your son? What had you planned to do with that twenty minutes?

Charles: My wife and I were going to watch a movie we had rented. And I was looking forward to having a little down time to just sit and relax.

Bernie: Maybe you also concluded that you wouldn't have the opportunity to relax?

Charles: That seems right. My wife and I haven't had the time to sit and watch a movie in weeks.

Throughout my session with Charles, I viewed myself as a partner in his self-exploration. I tried to be compassionate and nonjudgmental as I encouraged and supported him with openness and curiosity.

Proceeding from Your Negative Feeling

Identifying your negative feelings first and then working backward is another approach to recognizing your appraisals. Ask yourself what you might have concluded to experience such feelings. For example, feeling devalued would suggest that your knee-jerk reaction might have been "He/she devalued me." If you felt anxious, you may have viewed a triggering event as threatening to your future security. If you experienced betrayal, perhaps you decided that the person involved was no longer your ally.

From the Feelings List in chapter 8, identify five negative feelings that often propel you into anger. Try to recall the events and appraisals that would yield such feelings. Completing this exercise can help you identify your most frequent appraisals.

Being Mindful of Judgment

Be mindful to distinguish whether you're looking at your thoughts through the eyes of your compassionate self or your critical self. Be mindful about quickly judging your appraisal as "silly," "stupid," or "nonsensical." Such judgment interferes with self-awareness and hinders your task. Understandably, many of your appraisals stem from your mind's attempts to protect you from harm. After all, you may conclude that important desires or needs are being challenged or thwarted. So, certainly, some of your immediate appraisals may not seem logical. The following dialogue shows our tendency to be judgmental.

> Bernie: You described a variety of emotions you experienced when your husband disagreed with you in front of his parents. You emphasized disappointment, hurt, disrespect, and frustration. This word may sound a little strong, but I'm wondering if you experienced it on even a slight level. I wonder if you felt betrayed and that you concluded that he betrayed you?
>
> Olga: No, that doesn't make sense. I know he loves me.
>
> Bernie: Appraisals may not always make sense. You may "know" he loves you but not always "feel" that he does. After all, we can experience betrayal even with people we love.
>
> Olga: Well, I hate to admit it. But, I do think I was embarrassed because I felt he was completely taking their side. That's silly.
>
> Bernie: Maybe to your rational mind, but a part of you may have felt differently on an emotional level.

Being mindful to what at first may seem contradictory, nonsensical, or uncomfortable requires an attitude of *welcoming awareness*, an openness to observe rather than to analyze.

Another Approach to Help You Identify Appraisals

An appraisal involves your initial thought(s)—the conclusion, the meaning, or an opinion that you form regarding an event. Completing the following sentences may offer another approach to identifying your appraisal:

1. When the triggering event happened, I concluded that _____ .

2. If he/she _____ ed, it means that he/she _____ .

3. If he/she _____ ed, it means that I _____ .

4. If I _____ ed, it means that I _____ .

5. If that happened, it means that _____ .

Promoting Mindfulness about Expectations

Healthy anger depends on recognizing and distinguishing between those expectations formed from rational thought and those mostly based on child logic. For example, you may expect your partner to be on time even though he or she hasn't been punctual for the past five years of your relationship. Or, you may expect your partner to show the same degree of conscientiousness that you do when cleaning your home, or expect him or her to show more interest in your hobbies. At times, it's helpful to review your history to see whether your expectations are realistic or unrealistic. You may decide that your expectations are reasonable. Unfortunately, what may seem reasonable to you may not be the case for others.

This doesn't mean you should give up hope. Rather, it suggests that whatever you've tried in the past hasn't yet satisfied your desires. Rigidly holding on to the same expectations only furthers your suffering and tendency to anger. You may need to find new strategies to help satisfy your desires or realize when you need to let the old strategies go.

Review the list of expectations in chapter 7 to help you identify your own expectations. Try to relate them to your specific situation.

Be Mindful of Thinking That Leads to Expectations and Appraisals That Foster Anger Arousal

Certain types of thinking and patterns of thinking can make us vulnerable to anger, especially when overly influenced by child logic. The following sections define key examples of such thinking.

Cognitive Distortions

In his best-selling book *Feeling Good*, psychologist David Burns draws on cognitive psychology when he discusses *cognitive distortions*, thoughts that reflect errors in judgment.[1] He emphasizes the role our thoughts play in influencing our feelings. Early on, cognitive theorists pointed out the power of thought over emotions but didn't highlight the fact that our emotions can have an impact on our thinking. As such, thoughts and emotions mutually influence our cognitive distortions. Review the distortions described below. Assess the degree to which they may affect your expectations and appraisals. Specifically, try to determine how much they may increase your sense of threat and intensify your negative emotions, including anger.

All-or-nothing thinking. Expectations and appraisals grounded in "all-or-nothing thinking" can fuel our quickness to anger. Such thinking is both global and rigid. It interferes with our openmindedness and ability to see the full details of a situation. It may also keep us from noticing anything that contradicts our perspective. Some thoughts that reflect all-or-nothing thinking include, "You either love me or you don't" and "You are either my friend or my enemy."

Listen to the language of your thoughts and what you say. Using words such as "always" and "never" often indicates all-or-nothing thinking. The more you think in such extremes, the more likely you are to experience a range of negative feelings, including depression, anxiety, shame, and anger. This especially holds true if you adopt this attitude to evaluate yourself. Such thoughts can contribute to judgments such as "If I'm not perfect, I must be a failure."

This type of black-and-white thinking undermines our ability to look at the big picture with compassion. It leaves little flexibility to acknowledge our complex natures. And it keeps us from remembering that we're so much more than any single behavior, in spite of what our child logic tells us.

All-or-nothing thinking often springs from anxiety and uncertainty. We feel the need to make sense of our experiences. This leads us to quickly label them and to ignore the details of what makes them unique. Thinking in terms of absolutes can help us achieve harmony within ourselves. Acknowledging the complexities of life can be confusing. Such thinking, however, fails to consider that much of life involves *gray areas*, situations that lack consistency or don't conform to any specific pattern. Global thinking hampers our awareness of the details of our internal experiences and of the world in which we live.

Expectations based on all-or-nothing thinking promote intense dissatisfaction and anger in any relationship. And they can be especially disruptive in a meaningful, personal relationship. "If you did that, then you obviously don't love me" is a thought that fails to recognize the reality of loving relationships. Unfortunately, even those who really love us may also disappoint and hurt us.

Keep the following thoughts in mind to be more attentive to all-or-nothing thinking:

1. You can be intelligent and still do something foolish.

2. You can deeply love someone and still become angry with him or her on occasion.

3. At times, others can be insensitive to you even if they care about you and want the best for you.

4. Some areas in your life may be going very well while others are going poorly.

5. Just because a part of your life is exceptionally challenging now doesn't mean it will always be that way.

6. We engage in many experiences that have both good and negative aspects.

All-or-nothing thinking can arouse our anger in a variety of ways. We tend to want to categorize our experiences to fit into either a round hole or square hole, when in fact they may fit into neither. Now that's a formula for frustration and anger!

Overgeneralization. In overgeneralization, we note a single negative event and then base a conclusion on it. For example, we may err while drawing a sketch and immediately decide we're a lousy artist. Or, we might watch someone's behavior and make huge generalizations about how he or she would behave in other situations. According to Burns, this form of thinking often leads to depression, but it can also cause us to form expectations that make us vulnerable to anger.

Overgeneralization may lead us to form conclusions based on too little information. To practice healthy anger, we must realize when our past experiences are overly influencing our current assumptions. We often form knee-jerk appraisals when we overgeneralize.

Bethany, a participant in one of my classes, was quick to conclude that her husband, Nathan, was angry with her. "He's always speaking in a loud voice," she said. Bethany came from a family that rarely discussed emotions, but when expressing anger they did so loudly and in a threatening manner. In contrast, Nathan came from a family that was loud and highly emotional in all of their interactions.

Irritated at his girlfriend, another participant, Jamal, told me, "I assume the worst any time she comes home late. I imagine that she's having more fun without me. Sometimes, I figure she doesn't want to come home." Such a conclusion may stem from distrust. It may be rooted in low self-esteem and child logic when appraising how others behave, especially those we want to love us the most.

I've worked with many adolescents who have said things like, "I'm having trouble playing this song. I should just give up the guitar." They had obviously become very disappointed and annoyed with themselves based on an overgeneralization that because they made mistakes, they'd never learn to play the guitar.

In the first example, Bethany's child logic constantly leads her to conclude that her husband's raised voice spells aggression. In this situation, her child logic helps protect her. This may have served her well as a child but does not do so in her marriage.

The second example shows Jamal overgeneralizing about feeling unlovable. Because Jamal is already quick to think he's unlovable, he jumps to conclusions that his girlfriend feels the same way about him.

And the third situation shows that many adolescents are quick to overgeneralize because they believe they should have no weaknesses. Such generalizations may also stem from their grandiose child logic, which believes that a person should be able to easily learn anything without enduring frustration.

Emotional reasoning. This type of cognitive distortion involves a tendency to think "I feel it, therefore it must be true." To a great extent, our child logic leads us to thoughts that reflect emotional reasoning. These may involve assertions such as: "I feel angry, so I have a right be angry." "I feel betrayed by my spouse, so she betrayed me." Or, "I feel devalued, so he devalued me."

Emotional reasoning can blind us to seeing any other evidence to the contrary. Unfortunately, this kind of mindlessness makes us prone to anger.

"Should" statements. As described in chapter 8, thinking "shouldy" thoughts about others or yourself shows how rigidly you're holding on to your internal blueprint of expectations. You use these thoughts to judge the thoughts, feelings, and behaviors of others and yourself.

The truth is that our "shoulds" form many of the expectations that make us prone to anger. People behave differently from each other. Each of us is unique in our particular way of meeting life's challenges. We all have our own likes and dislikes. And yet, because we can't see beyond our own perspectives, we all too often judge others as being wrong. These inflexible thinking patterns influence our appraisals regarding others and ourselves, with or without our awareness. They leave us vulnerable to threatening and negative feelings, both of which can lead to anger.

Personalization. In personalization, you quickly blame yourself for a negative event even when you weren't solely responsible. This tendency can arouse anger within you and others. This is just another example of a person embracing tough love rather than self-compassion.

Other Attitudes That Negatively Affect Expectations and Appraisals

In addition to the forms of cognitive distortion discussed by Burns, some other thoughts and attitudes clearly have an impact on both expectations and appraisals. Some of these may go hand in hand with the distortions already identified. Others reflect more global thinking.

Perfectionism. Rigidly expecting to be perfect is destructive in many ways, but some perfectionism can be constructive. For example, it's rewarding to score perfectly on a test, to perfectly perform a musical piece, or to make a hole in one. Success gives us a sense of gratification after all of our hard work while we are learning and polishing our skills. It gives us joy.

Healthy perfectionism means setting high standards for ourselves while knowing full well that perfectionism in most areas of our lives isn't realistic. This can help us persist when facing a challenge or focus our attention so that we do better at a task. Healthy perfectionism can help us push ourselves beyond our normal comfort zones to achieve our goals. While it may involve competing with others, it usually means measuring our goals against our own past performance.

And healthy perfectionism requires us to be self-compassionate when we fail to achieve our goals. Rather than criticizing ourselves, such compassion means wisely identifying the obstacles we face and thinking about what we might do differently in the future. Self-compassion also helps us determine whether our goals were realistic to begin with.

Certainly, we may become disappointed or frustrated when we fail to be perfect. This can lead to low-level irritation. Such a reaction is usually mild, however, compared with the anger of *maladaptive perfectionism*.

Trying to compensate for feelings of inadequacy sometimes leads to unhealthy perfectionism. This may be driven by a need to avoid the threat of criticism, rejection, or shame. Instead of running toward a goal, we try to run away from our discomfort.

Some people may experience intense anxiety when their attempts at perfection are blocked or thwarted. Such perfectionism is a way to boost our self-esteem when we fear feeling like a failure or even a "nothing." We may view any imperfection within ourselves as a threat to our self-esteem or worth. This leads us to make knee-jerk negative appraisals that leave us vulnerable to anger, especially with ourselves.

We may become angry with ourselves when we fail to meet goals such as learning a new skill, playing a sport, or beginning a new career. These feelings can arise when we set our expectations too high. Some people never start their journey. Others become paralyzed by perfectionism and lose the motivation to finish reaching their goals. Some quit at the slightest feelings of inadequacy. Others fail to take the final steps necessary to complete their journey. And many perfectionists won't tolerate anything less than perfection in others.

A client of mine had an older sister who was a highly successful swimmer on her high school team. On one occasion, my client competed against and outperformed her. Her sister felt so defeated that the next day, she quit the team and vowed never to swim again. Her decision showed the anger she felt toward herself for failing to meet her expectations. It was a decision based on tough love and her inability to accept that she couldn't always be the best.

The need to be right. There's no arguing that we tend to feel good when we're right about an issue. Being right validates us at a deep level. Being right helps us feel accepted and boosts our self-confidence. We may feel right about something we say, an action we take, or a fact that we know.

Feeling compelled to be right, however, has an entirely different impact on our lives. Such a need becomes an obsession that drains us and leads us to unrealistic expectations and appraisals. We may spend a great deal of energy and time trying to be right in the eyes of others and ourselves.

This may sound obvious, but our fear of being wrong compels our need to be right. What may not be obvious is the intensely negative feelings that come from being wrong. The drive to avoid feeling the shame, rejection, inadequacy, or sense of failure or vulnerability that we experience when we're wrong fuels the need to be right. This is an extremely high bar to set for ourselves. It invariably leads to self-consciousness, withdrawal, and self-criticism. And, as with the need to be perfect, the need to be right reflects a harsh tough-love mindset.

Beliefs of entitlement. Some people's sense of entitlement makes them more vulnerable to the rapid arousal of anger. They have inappropriate and unrealistic expectations that circumstances and other people should treat them favorably. They often take the attitude that they're special and that others should treat them as such. People with this attitude may assume they shouldn't have to experience frustration. They may believe that their needs and desires take precedence over others'. It's this aspect of entitle-ment that most often contributes to anger.

Child logic clearly influences our sense of entitlement. These self-absorbed thoughts and attitudes reduce our ability to show compassion to others. They also make it very difficult to distinguish a need from a desire, making us especially vulnerable to anger.

The belief that life is or should be fair. Believing that life should be fair lays the foundation for a great amount of anger. It's rooted in child logic that fails to recognize that life isn't fair. It ignores the fact that being human means we suffer sometimes, regardless of who we are or how we've lived our lives.

We may suffer from illness, financial difficulties, loss, relationship con-flicts, or other traumatic experiences. And some of us suffer more than others. This is a part of being human. Rigidly believing that life should be fair only increases our suffering and anger. As Rabbi Harold Kushner emphasized, bad things can happen to good people. And sometimes good things happen to bad people.[2]

For example, you may believe you'll be immune to illness if you eat the right foods, exercise, and get enough sleep. But while these behaviors increase your chances of good health, they don't guarantee it. Similarly, you may believe that if you commit to practicing good deeds, good things should always come your way. While you may increase the likelihood that this will happen, you can't guarantee it. Likewise, you may experience suf-fering in your life regardless of your religion and how you practice it.

Confusing what you desire with what you really need. We become much more vulnerable to anger when we believe that our wishes are needs. This lowers our threshold for experiencing threatening and negative feelings, which may include hurt, disappointment, and sadness. Our most basic needs are those that sustain life, such as food, clothing, and shelter. Other desires that come close to being needs include our social connections, money, and perhaps a means of transportation to get to work. Everything else is a want or a desire. While these may improve the quality of our lives, they aren't essential. Unfortunately, many of us believe we *need* a particular object, a certain event to occur, or someone to behave in a certain way.

I'm not suggesting you give up your desires for a more fulfilling life. As we saw in earlier chapters, your brain has developed, in part, to help move you in this direction. But the more you define happiness by the fulfillment of wants rather than needs, the more quickly you'll grow angry when such desires remain unsatisfied.

For example, it's natural to want approval from others and to enjoy a strong bond with those we care about. But many of us believe we need everyone to accept and love us. This may be due to a lack of self-confidence, strong dependency needs, or insecurity. So, while we may feel we need everyone to respect, admire, or even approve of us, we don't need this. Each time you label a want a need, you're rigidly maintaining a "should" in your expectations, whether for others or yourself.

Too often inhabiting a "time zone" other than the present. On a given day, your mind may wander to a variety of concerns. But which "time zone" most preoccupies your thoughts—the past, the present, or the future? When you take your daily mind-body pulse—which you learned to do in chapter 3—be mindful to observe which time period your thoughts reside in most often.

Focusing on the future can pull us into the future. Setting goals for the future gives us meaning and enriches our lives. It offers us direction and a sense of empowerment and control. With that said, it's possible to focus too much on the future, whether the next few days, weeks, months, or years. We may be so preoccupied with envisioning our future happiness that we fail to create joy in our present lives. Worry or fear about the future may lead us to spend an extraordinary amount of energy trying to control it.

In contrast, we may focus on the past. It's certainly helpful to explore the past so as to make informed choices in the present. We may look back with nostalgia at the positive relationships and experiences we've had throughout the years. Doing so with appreciation offers us a sense of history that nurtures and fulfills us. And, certainly, we may need to mourn and grieve past hurts in order to move on, which supports our emotional well-being. A preoccupation with the past, however, may lead us to view all that occurs in our life through past events. And if we've had difficulties in the past, we may be especially prone to seeing threats in our current life where none exist.

By predominantly living in the past or the future, we spend too much time living in our heads. Worrying about the future or dwelling on the past creates a formula for anxiety and depression. It keeps us from being in the present and enjoying the life we're living now.

* * *

This chapter has focused on being mindful of patterns in your thinking and attitudes that may make you vulnerable to anger. The next chapter introduces practices that will help you more readily observe, sit with, and manage the reactions, feelings, and thoughts that are a part of anger arousal.

For Further Reflection

1. What is your relationship with your child logic? How comfortable are you when you realize that emotions dominate some of your thinking? Are you embarrassed when you observe such thoughts? If so, you'll find that self-compassion can help address these reactions.

2. Which cognitive distortions characterize your thinking? Do you know how you came to think in such a way?

3. How much of a perfectionist are you? Are you a perfectionist in some areas but not in others? If you're a perfectionist, how much is healthy versus unhealthy?

4. How strongly does your need to be right lead to conflict with others and with yourself? Do you know how you came to have such strict expectations of yourself?

5. What messages did you learn as a child regarding the notion that life should be fair?

6. To what degree are you preoccupied with the past or the future? If you believe your thoughts leave the present too often, try to become mindful of the triggers that shift your focus and attention.

CHAPTER 11

Self-Compassion for Healthy Anger

The practices described in this chapter are based on the lessons you've learned up to this point. They'll help you use self-compassion in every aspect of your anger arousal. The most important step in this process is showing compassion for your hurting self.

As confirmed by research in compassion-focused therapy, self-compassion is expressed in the dialogue, or *self-talk*, that you have with yourself. It means mindfully engaging in self-talk originating from your compassionate self and directed toward your suffering self. This self-talk forms from a mind-body state of safety and calm. It focuses on sitting with your pain as a way of moving past it.

Directing Compassion at Your Hurting Self

Anger and the feelings that surround it are accompanied by great emotional and physical discomfort. Whereas mindfulness reduces the intensity of your reactions, self-compassion offers empathy to the suffering part of you. The following exercise will help you more easily evoke your compassionate self to soothe your anguish when feeling anger.

> **EXERCISE**
>
> *Practicing Compassion toward Your Experience of Anger*
>
> First, complete an Anger Log about an incident that made you angry. Then find a place where you can sit comfortably without being

disturbed. Gently close your eyes and engage in mindfulness breathing for a few moments.

Next, do the exercise(s) from chapter 5 that most powerfully arouse(s) your compassionate self. Sit with this self for a few moments.

Picture a version of yourself sitting a few feet in front of you. This is the part of you that feels threatened and angry. It's also the part of you that may feel sad, ignored, rejected, shamed, or any negative feeling underlying anger. Envision a version of yourself as you are now or as you were at a past time in your life. You may find viewing a photo of yourself helpful for this.

Now imagine that you're experiencing emotional pain from the triggering event in your Anger Log. Just sit and observe yourself for a moment. Note how your facial expression, posture, and overall demeanor show your suffering. Envision yourself simply saying, "I feel [anger and other negative feeling(s)]."

Your sole focus at this moment is to direct compassion toward your hurting self. Express your compassion in the following ways:

1. *Use phrases.*
   - I'm here to sit with you and your anger.
   - I'm here to sit with you and your pain.
   - This is what you are feeling right now.
   - Let's just stay with it for a while.
   - I know it's uncomfortable.
   - We don't need to act right now.
   - I know you can manage this.
   - I'm here.
   - You may feel like you can't handle this, but I'll help you.
   - I won't leave you.
   - I'm just sitting here with you.

2. *Use facial expressions.* Envision making a facial expression that shows warmth and genuine compassion to your hurting self.

3. *Make eye contact.* Eye contact genuinely connects us with one another. Envision moving close to and looking into the eyes of your hurting self.

4. *Check your posture.* Imagine leaning forward, being there for and attentive to your hurting self.

5. *Make physical contact.* Picture yourself making physical contact in a compassionate way. For example, you may want to imagine placing your hand on the head or shoulder of your hurting self, or simply holding his or her hand.

This exercise can help you see your compassionate self as distinctly separate from your hurting self. It's about sitting with and witnessing your anguish without attempting to fix it. It's about increasing your tolerance of and comfort with your internal experiences.

Self-Compassion toward Your Thoughts

Healthy anger means realizing and accepting that our emotional brains may influence and distort our expectations and appraisals. Recognizing our expectations and appraisals as they unfold depends on observing and responding to them with compassion.

The following statements show compassion toward your hurting self's distorted or unrealistic expectations and appraisals. Each expresses acceptance of these expectations and appraisals. And they all indicate that it's natural to have such reactions, given your unique history.

Of course your thoughts go in this direction, given your past.

It figures.

There it goes again.

It makes perfect sense to your emotional brain.

This is what I'm thinking right now.

That's a familiar path.

You'll find the following self-compassionate responses helpful when you want to let go of certain expectations:

If only it were true.

How nice that would be.

It is unfortunate, disappointing, and sad that life [he, she, the situation, the world] isn't the way I would like it to be.

Evoking Your Compassionate Wisdom

Evoke your compassionate wisdom (see chapter 4) to answer the following questions about your appraisals:

1. How accurate was my appraisal?

2. What other appraisals would I have formed if I were in a different emotional state?

3. What four appraisals could I have made to explain the event—appraisals that had nothing to do with me?

4. What can I do if my appraisal is true?

5. What might I suggest to a best friend in the same situation?

Self-Compassion toward Needs and Wants

Being self-compassionate means feeling empathy and sympathy for ourselves when we realize a certain desire may go unsatisfied. While it's natural to experience sadness and suffering when facing this fact, showing compassion to your grieving self and mourning your unmet desires is a large part of letting go of anger.

The following are compassionate responses to your hurting self when your needs or desires go unmet:

It's sad to give up your desires. I'll sit with you, with your sadness.

Unfortunately, you may feel or believe your desire is a need when it's not.

I'm here to help you meet your needs.

I'll help take care of you.

I'm here to help you grieve.

What do you really need?

Compassionate Acceptance of the Experience as a Whole

You can incorporate the following statements into your self-talk to show compassionate acceptance of the situation:

Life can be challenging, and I'll face this situation in the best way I can.

Whatever I'm experiencing now is what I experience.

I'm capable of experiencing what I experience and doing what needs to be done.

I'll accept my contribution to my anger.

I'll accept my past.

The more often you fill out the Anger Log and respond to every aspect of your experience with self-compassion, the more you'll be able to do the same when responding to triggering events in real life.

The Practice of Self-Compassion: A Vignette

The following vignette demonstrates the practices outlined so far. It shows the role that validation, empathy, and sympathy play when being self-compassionate with our anger.

I greeted Dylan in the waiting room. I immediately sensed his intensity from his firm handshake and his tight facial muscles. Even his "hello" seemed tense as he entered my office with a slow and heavy gait. He was well over six feet tall, in his thirties, and appeared solid. His entire body conveyed resentment at being referred for my services.

Dylan was yet another client told by his company to seek anger management counseling. He described a string of incidents marked by escalating anger—each one worse than the last. Although they had occurred over a two-year period, his latest outburst had pushed his supervisor's patience.

Dylan was married, with two young children. His wife was a stay-at-home mom but was now looking for work to help their financial situation. Dylan had worked for his company, which specialized in information technology, for seven years. Before that, he'd worked at a small company that had abruptly closed down.

Initially, Dylan was extremely pleased with his work. But over time, he became increasingly disgruntled. The company had lied to him about the travel requirements when he took the job. Now, he resented having to travel so much. He felt unsupported and unrecognized and believed his salary was too low. During previous anger incidents, he had raised his voice to a supervisor and to coworkers. During the latest exchange, Dylan not only raised his voice to his supervisor but also cursed and then abruptly stood up, accidentally knocking his chair over. Dylan then slammed his hand down on the supervisor's desk.

The triggering event for Dylan's anger was a report from his supervisor. It showed that one of Dylan's clients had given him negative feedback, and as a result, the supervisor had immediately removed Dylan from the account without calling him first to discuss it.

After several of our sessions, Dylan acknowledged a number of concerns that increased his tendency to become angry. His recent history played a huge role. Dylan still harbored anger related to losing his previous position. He felt that the company had deceived him regarding its financial status. When the company shut down without warning, Dylan and his wife had a one-year-old child and were expecting another. They had recently purchased a new home.

Dylan's current supervisor had been in the position for only two years. He had different expectations that clearly clashed with Dylan's. Following extensive self-reflection and practice completing the Anger Log, Dylan provided the responses shown in table 11.1.

More recently, tensions had increased when Dylan's wife decided to return to work only part-time. He immediately became anxious about the financial burden this might create.

I first shared with Dylan the framework of anger and practices in mindfulness and self-compassion. He completed the Anger Log regarding the incident that led to his referral, and I then helped him to engage in the following practices of self-compassion.

Table 11.1. Dylan's Responses on the Anger Log

Motivating forces	→	Expectations	→	Triggering event	→	Appraisals	→	Negative feelings	→	Anger intensity (on a scale of 1 to 10)
Desire for honesty, respect, recognition, financial security, stability		My supervisor should respect me and be honest with me. I will have minimal travel.		He made a decision without telling me.		I can't trust him. He doesn't respect me. I could lose my job. I will have increased financial pressure. I made the wrong decision by taking this job.		Betrayed Distrustful Anxious Disrespected Powerless Deceived		9

Bodily reactions: Tension in chest and arms; feeling warmer; increased rate of breathing

Self-talk: I can't believe this guy. I should just quit. I really would like to hit him. I hate being this angry.

Images: Shoving everything on the supervisor's desk onto the floor

Previous events and mood prior to triggering event: History of feeling deceived and betrayed at work and in past experiences outside work

Practicing self-compassion for his body and negative feelings, including anger. For Dylan, self-compassion began with recognizing the physical discomfort associated with anger and the feelings of betrayal, anxiety, disrespect, and powerlessness behind it. He also evoked his compassionate self, practiced mindfulness breathing, and reduced his muscle tension. These practices helped him sit with his anguish. As a result, he felt less threatened and fearful about losing his job.

Practicing self-compassion led Dylan to see that his feelings were only temporary and that he didn't have to act on them. He realized that he used his anger to distract himself from past hurts. He became alert to the fact that criticizing himself for getting angry only worsened the negative feelings of anger, anxiety, guilt, and shame.

At such moments, Dylan compassionately told himself, "I know it's uncomfortable, but I'll sit here with you. I'll help calm you, but right now you're feeling tension and hurt." "We can handle this. We can just sit here with these feelings. Right now you're feeling anger and tension." He also practiced meditation to relax his body.

Practicing self-compassion for his appraisals. As part of being self-compassionate, Dylan became more mindful of his appraisals. He talked to that part of himself that was upset or scared. Careful to avoid judgments, he addressed each appraisal of his supervisor or his job in the following ways:

Thought: I can't trust him.

It's understandable you would think that right now.

What is his history regarding being trustworthy?

What other factors could have contributed to his decision to take you off the account?

What is your history with trusting people?

What is the nature of the client's needs?

Thought: He doesn't respect me.

It's understandable you would think that right now.

How respectful has he been in the past?

What other reasons may have led him to take you off the account without telling you?

You may simply have different expectations that lead to conflict.

Thought: I could lose my job.

It's understandable that you may think that.

How have your evaluations been in the past?

What is the real likelihood of that happening?

Even if that happened, I'll take care of you.

Thought: I will have increased financial pressure.

You've been preoccupied with this for some time.

It makes sense that you would have this thought as one of your first knee-jerk appraisals.

There are things I can do to reduce your pressure.

I can work on identifying these things to reduce your pressure.

Thought: I made the wrong decision in taking this job.

This is a thought you come to when you're scared and frustrated, so it makes sense you would think this.

You made the decision with the awareness you had at the time.

Be mindful to avoid beating yourself up about insights you didn't have at the time.

By being a wise parent to himself, Dylan was able to consider alternative thoughts to his immediate appraisals.

Practicing self-compassion for his expectations. Consistent with being compassionate toward each element that contributed to his anger, Dylan was encouraged to respond to his hurting self in the following ways:

It's disappointing when our expectations are not satisfied.

We sometimes maintain expectations even when they are not realistic.

It certainly would feel much better if people behaved the way I wish they would. Unfortunately, they behave as they see fit to behave.

Perhaps my boss was feeling pressured by others.	Maybe you (we) need to work at letting go of some expectations.
Actually, he's not always been honest.	Maybe I need to be more flexible in my expectations.
People are human.	

Dylan recognized that self-compassion is essential for the grieving and mourning that goes along with changing or completely letting go of certain expectations.

Practicing self-compassion for his needs and desires. Self-compassion, for Dylan, required him to evoke his wisdom to better understand his needs and desires. He noted that while he felt threatened about lacking the money essential to meeting his needs, most of his feelings of threat arose in relation to his desires. Recognizing this distinction was a major component of Dylan's self-compassion. Thinking about what he could do to address his needs and desires also called on the wisdom of his compassionate self.

Dylan decided to be assertive and ask his supervisor why he had removed him from the account without speaking to him first. After thinking about it, Dylan recalled similar incidences. He realized that his expectations of honesty from his supervisor were unrealistic. Dylan would also inquire of his supervisor what degree of honesty he could expect in the future.

Further, Dylan realized that he needed to talk with his wife about his anxiety regarding their finances. He hadn't been candid with her about his feelings and expectations surrounding the topic of money. They both realized they needed to discuss their path to financial security.

Mindfulness about Your Various "Selves"

Dylan's story shows how evoking our most compassionate selves can assist us in addressing pain. It also illustrates how we, as humans, have multiple "selves," each with a broad variety of motivations. For example, one part may occasionally seek out social interaction while another craves moments of solitude. Similarly, one part can be entirely serious and focused on the task at hand while another enjoys playfully engaging in leisure activities.

In a sense, being truly mindful of your "selves" involves being mindful of which self you let flourish. During mindfulness, you're free to create and expand your identity. Your observing self can be mindful of your thoughts and feelings and can actively choose which to embrace and which to let go. In effect, this is the moment of truth in which you can nurture your self-compassionate self and, by doing so, decide how you want to live your life.

Loving-Kindness Meditation

Loving-kindness meditation involves having a talk with yourself that reflects tenderness, love, and friendliness. Sharon Salzberg, cofounder of the Insight Meditation Society, highlights using such practices for cultivating both self-compassion and compassion for others.[1] The following phrases are part of compassion-focused practices and meditations:[2]

May I be free from danger.

May I have mental happiness.

May I have physical happiness.

May I have ease of well-being.

Such loving-kindness can be expressed during moments of hurt, as well as at other times. These meditations are intended to show our goodwill, especially when evoked from our compassionate selves.

You may feel awkward or even silly at first when doing these meditations. They may make you uncomfortable, or they may have no emotional impact at all. However, like the other practices in this chapter, repeating them can increasingly help you go from thinking you should be self-compassionate to feeling self-compassionate.

Forgiveness as a Compassionate Response to Anger

Forgiveness is an essential part of healthy anger. It's something we do to help ourselves and ease our suffering. And whether we just forgive someone in our mind or actually articulate it, we're expressing compassion. By choosing forgiveness, we can begin to cultivate *forgivingness*, a willingness to forgive. Forgivingness can affect our expectations and appraisals, reducing our potential for anger and helping us move past it.

The Meaning and Purpose of Forgiveness

With forgiveness, a person gradually lets go of resentment that results from wishing or expecting that the past could have been different. It means getting over the anger related to past hurts or blame. It requires a person to grieve and fully accept when nothing can be done to undo what's already happened.

Forgiveness doesn't mean ignoring or minimizing suffering. It doesn't mean that intellectually understanding our hurts substitutes for feeling them. In fact, we can't truly forgive and move on until we've fully recognized and experienced our pain. It doesn't mean we condone the behavior that caused our suffering or allow it to continue. Practicing forgiveness doesn't suggest we put ourselves in harm's way. Nor does it necessarily involve reconciling with the person who hurt us, although it may lead to that.

Suffering is a natural part of life. All of us have experienced hurt in various ways—some much more than others. And while we can't undo these events, embracing forgiveness is a way to let go of the pain.

There is no set time frame for forgiveness. Forgiveness is a process. Forgiveness may require just simple and brief reflection. Or, forgiveness may take months or even years as we try to move past the hurtful experience. We may view certain acts as unforgivable, even while we work at forgivingness.

Benefits of Forgiveness

Cultivating forgiveness releases us from the draining thoughts and feelings of resentment and revenge. It can have a profound impact on our lives.

- Studies show that forgiveness is related to greater emotional health, including less anger, anxiety, and depression and a greater satisfaction with life.[3]
- Forgiveness frees us to trust and connect with others. And it makes us more likely to invest emotionally in our relationships.
- Forgiveness benefits our physical health.[4–6]
- Studies suggest that forgiveness in our most intimate relationship leads to improved conflict resolution and greater satisfaction.[7]
- The ability to forgive strengthens commitment in relationships and can decrease anxieties about loss and abandonment.
- Forgiveness decreases human suffering.

Forgiveness as an Act of Self-Compassion

Our capacity to make peace with another person and with the world
depends very much on our capacity to make peace with ourselves.
—Thich Nhat Hanh

Forgiveness is something we do to help ourselves heal from our hurts, whether our own words or actions or those of others. It's an act of self-compassion. Without self-forgiveness, we stay resentful with ourselves. Resentment can lead to self-loathing as well as toxic guilt and shame.

Self-forgiveness involves letting go of self-critical and harsh judgments: thoughts that foster toxic guilt or shame and underlie depression. Self-forgiveness doesn't mean we deny our responsibility for certain actions but rather that we view them as part of being human. Such compassion comes from our wisdom, which reminds us to be mindful about making better choices in the future.

Forgiveness of others requires us to be compassionate with them—not because of what they did, but for who they are. At times, forgiving others may seem more like a hope than a reality.

General Guidelines for Promoting Forgivingness

All of the practices in this book support the cultivation of forgiveness. They enable you to recognize, sit with, and move past suffering. With that said, cultivating *forgivingness* requires self-awareness and mindfulness. It requires you to fully explore and move past your most significant wounds.

All too often, your inability to move past your hurts can lead you to experience new triggering events. You may impulsively think, "It's happening again," during one of your knee-jerk appraisals of a potentially triggering event. Whether you're fully aware of these experiences in your mind or just in your body, this message from your past demands your attention.

Specific Practices for Forgiveness

A variety of strategies and insights can help you expand your capacity for forgivingness.

Identify your baseline regarding forgiveness. It will be helpful for you to determine your baseline level of forgiveness: the degree to which you're forgiving in general. Before beginning the more formal practices in the

rest of this chapter, complete the Heartland Forgiveness Scale at www
.heartlandforgiveness.com, then periodically complete the scale to determine your progress.

Look for patterns in your responses to the Anger Log. Review your responses in the Anger Logs that you've completed. Look for patterns or
themes that may reflect sensitivity regarding specific desires. How might
these be a reaction to past hurts? Perhaps you most often value a desire
for connection or respect, or recognition or security, or perhaps trust or
justice. Although most of us experience these desires, they grow in importance when you've suffered frequent or severe hurts. They may make you
vulnerable to unforgivingness.

Review your expectations and appraisals. Look for patterns in your appraisals. You may realize that you're quick to believe someone will harm
you. Or, you may tend to form an appraisal implying abandonment or betrayal or rejection where none was intended. On occasion, you may project
these motivations onto others when in fact you harbor these feelings or
thoughts toward *them.*

Review your negative feelings. Observe patterns in your negative feelings
and the related sense of threat that makes you angry. These may be key
sensitivities that deserve attention or may be residue from hurtful events
that requires self-compassion. Perhaps you're quick to feel anxiety, fear,
worthlessness, self-doubt, isolation, or rejection. Each feeling that you experience frequently or intensely can help you plan further self-compassion
and forgiveness work.

Take a closer look at your hurt. Recognizing and letting go of your most
severe hurts can be one of the most difficult challenges to embracing
healthy anger and forgivingness. You can use the Anger Log to help you
accomplish this task.

Completing an Anger Log on Your Most Severe Hurts

For your most severe hurts, completion of an Anger Log can help you
clearly define the most complex emotions and thoughts surrounding these
experiences and help you move past them.

Complete a log for each person who has hurt you. The log should reflect some significant interaction or patterns of interaction that caused
your pain. Begin with those individuals who caused you the least harm and

gradually proceed to those who have hurt you the most. Deal with one hurt at a time, whether it takes days, weeks, or longer. Be mindful to describe specific observable behaviors.

For example, suppose that while growing up, your brother routinely made you feel devalued. The triggering event might simply be stated as, "He frequently criticized or ridiculed me." Or, if your parent was emotionally unavailable, your triggering event might be stated as, "She wasn't available to discuss or help me understand my feelings."

Identify the key desires that you had with regard to these individuals. Identify your expectations of them, the appraisals you formed, and the feelings you experienced. It takes great courage to do this, but it's empowering to clearly describe the full experience. The completed log is a clearly stated summary of your grievance. It's a meaningful step toward letting go of your hurt and embracing forgivingness.

Remember that forgiveness often moves in baby steps. It's a process that takes time. You may find it helpful to share your experience with a close friend, a loved one, or a professional.

Self-Inquiry for Forgiveness

Answering the following questions can help you release your resentment toward those who have caused you the most suffering.

1. Realistically, could I have done anything to increase the likelihood that I could have changed his or her behavior? If so, is my belief based on hindsight rather than on insight I didn't possess at the time?

2. If I could have acted differently and resent myself for that, how can I now forgive myself?

3. Is there anything I can do now to change that situation?

Sitting With and Moving Past Pain

The strategies presented in this book so far offer a range of practices to help you sit with and move past the pain and discomfort associated with anger. The following is a summary of these strategies—some guidelines to remember:

1. Be mindful that suffering is a natural part of fully engaging in life.
2. We must first acknowledge and experience pain in order to heal.
3. Pain needs to be labeled as accurately as possible.
4. The intensity of emotional suffering reduces over time.

When the Emotional Pain Feels Overwhelming

Self-compassion involves being mindful of and attentive to your discomfort during and after your experience of anger. Self-compassion also means recognizing when the pain feels too overwhelming to sit with. Here are some ways to help address such anguish:

1. Sit and engage in mindfulness breathing.
2. Do the physical relaxation exercises described in chapter 6.
3. Picture yourself in your safe and peaceful place.
4. Engage in a nurturing activity that consumes your attention. This could be physical exercise, reading a novel, enjoying your favorite hobby, writing, listening to comforting music, watching a movie, or simply taking a bath.
5. Seek out those who are genuinely supportive and loving. While you may want their advice or encouragement, you occasionally might just wish to share time together and savor your connection with them.
6. Imagine yourself in the near future, looking back on this event through the eyes of your compassionate self. What would you tell yourself about the situation?
7. When necessary, seek counseling to deal with your pain; this is just another form of self-compassion—one that can provide you with additional support and strategies for your unique situation.

Grieving and Mourning

Grieving and mourning are key components of self-compassion that arise after we have let go of anger. Grieving means fully acknowledging the feelings about a loss, such as anger, fear, or sadness. Mourning involves the ongoing process of adapting to a life that doesn't include whoever or whatever is being mourned. With regard to anger, mourning is letting go of unrealistic expectations, like the belief that we shouldn't get ill or suffer. It calls for us to be mindful of when it's in our best interest to let go of unsatisfied desires or unmet goals. This is no small feat. It involves ongoing moments of finding comfort as we deal with the loss of what we'd hoped for. Mourning takes time and is a major component of healthy anger. The practices in this chapter will guide you through this process.

*   *   *

This chapter has provided strategies to help you practice compassion in every aspect of your anger experience. The next two chapters focus on showing compassion to others, which is essential to self-compassion and healthy anger.

For Further Reflection

1. What are some of the main expectations that derive from your child logic? Identify several self-compassionate responses that can help soothe you when these expectations are threatened or unsatisfied.

2. What motivating forces have you believed to be needs but, upon reflection, recognize as desires? Answering this question requires you to be fully honest with yourself.

3. Being mindful of your thoughts requires paying attention to the appraisals that you make without full information. How rigid are you in forming personalized, knee-jerk reactions without considering alternative explanations for how others behave? What has contributed to your tendency to do this?

4. It's self-compassionate to be mindful that although others may or may not be available to help us, we are ultimately our own best, wise, and nurturing caretakers. Ask yourself the following questions, some of which are based on practices in Robin Casarjian's book *Forgiveness:*[8]

    a. Do you want your parents' (or anyone else's) unconditional love?

    b. Have you been willing to love them unconditionally?

    c. Do you want their approval?

    d. Have you been willing to accept them as they are?

    e. How easy is it to give to others what you most want from them?

5. Cultivating self-compassion to practice healthy anger depends on being mindful of criticizing ourselves. Try to be attentive to thoughts that reflect tough love. Record them when they occur, either on paper or on your computer. Then think of a self-compassionate thought you might use instead. Be mindful about practicing the alternative thought and frequently reviewing your list.

6. You might identify an alternative compassionate thought in the following ways:

   a. Identify what you would compassionately say to your best friend who is dealing with the same situation.

   b. What would one of the members of your visualized group of compassionate people say to you about your situation?

   c. What would you want a most compassionate and loving parent to say to you about your situation?

PART III

Healing Relationships by Changing the Anger Response

CHAPTER 12

Mindfulness, Self-Compassion, and Compassion for Others

Showing compassion to others kindles the same sense of connection, warmth, and safety within us that we feel when practicing compassion toward ourselves. As such, compassion for others is also an act of self-compassion.[1] People differ in their ability to show compassion. Some seem to ration it out. Others show compassion only to children, elderly people, or animals. And still others may be more compassionate to men than to women, or vice versa.

With or without our awareness, we each live by unspoken rules that decide who *deserves* our compassion. Some people may show more compassion to someone stricken with stomach cancer, with no known cause, than to someone with lung cancer that results from smoking. Others think that those who seem to have caused their own suffering warrant less compassion than "true" victims. This attitude is common toward those with AIDS, HIV, or substance addiction. Such judgment focuses on behavior rather than on suffering. It competes with being compassionate and is the opposite of genuine compassion. It blinds us to recognizing and accepting that we're all flawed and weak in some way.

Just like anger, our openness to showing compassion depends on our habits of thinking, feeling, and behaving. Consequently, cultivating compassion requires practice, patience, and commitment.

Many of us find it much easier to be compassionate with others than with ourselves. Some people may feel motivated to be compassionate because they genuinely accept humanity and want to alleviate suffering. A compulsion to be good, nice, or self-sacrificing may fuel the practice of compassion. Sometimes, compassion is an effort to gain acceptance. Many people measure their overall self-worth through the eyes of others or possibly even a God. They may also practice compassion to receive praise or a reward—even salvation.

Genuine compassion is rooted in accepting ourselves and others. It's not something we do primarily for acceptance by others. To cultivate compassion for others, we must keep our shared humanity in mind. We all have habits regarding our emotions, thoughts, and sensations, and many people function—to some degree—while ignoring their habits. Similarly, everyone has hot buttons that make them vulnerable to anger. And everyone carries within themselves a blueprint of their desires and expectations in life. We all want to feel safe, connected, and fulfilled.

Fostering compassion for others means being mindful of their internal experiences—without judgment. It requires knowing who they are inside rather than looking at their behaviors alone. This involves mindfully observing their words, their facial expressions, and their tone of voice as well as what they're actually saying.

Compassion toward other people depends on being mindful of your thoughts concerning them and your interactions with them. Although actions can cultivate compassion to some extent, it's more often the case that, as psychologist Christopher Germer put it, "changing our relationships to the people in our heads is the first step toward working with them in real time."[2]

The Obstacles to Being Compassionate to Others

What are you feeling at this moment? What are you thinking right now? What are you experiencing in your body right now? Take some time to be mindful of these experiences before you continue reading.

You may feel warmth and contentment as you read about showing compassion to others. Or you might feel uncomfortable. Perhaps you've decided that practicing compassion is beyond your reach and that only saints or the very spiritual can do it. You may feel shame or guilt if you haven't shown enough compassion to others. You may also feel threatened at the very thought of showing compassion to others, fearing it will leave you vulnerable to harm.

You may face some unique challenges when offering compassion to others, which may include one or more of the following (I'll use examples to illustrate some of these):

Thinking you should be compassionate to others is different from feeling *compassion for others.* Be mindful of your motivations to be compassionate. Identify those stemming from a desire for praise or reward and those that come from within you. As with self-compassion, you may initially *think* that you should be compassionate toward others before you *feel* that you should.

You may view compassion as a limited resource. Wade was a young man who sought my help for anger and low-level depression. After thinking about it, he realized that he believed showing compassion to others would keep him from satisfying his own needs and desires. He viewed compassion as finite and limited, like the pieces of a pie. He had always been cautious about being compassionate with others. In fact, he often felt drained when he practiced compassion.

Wade had ignored his needs and desires in past relationships. He felt compelled to do so. As a sensitive child, he grew up overly aware of his parents' pain. He believed himself responsible for alleviating it and sometimes even for causing it. Wade allowed these types of thoughts to affect many of his adult relationships. Unfortunately, they were a potent contribution to both his depression and his related anger.

You are familiar only with who you believe others are. Cultivating compassion for other people requires us to be open to seeing them as they really are rather than as we want to see them. We may be inclined to see only their strengths and stay blind to their suffering. Or, when viewing them through anger, we may focus only on their behaviors rather than on connecting with them on a deeper level.

Reflecting on the suffering of others may lead you to experience discomfort. Our ability to witness and sit with our own pain enables us to feel the suffering of others. But if you try to avoid experiencing your own pain, you may find it difficult to be empathetic with others. You may just conclude that they need to be tougher or that they are self-indulgent when they even acknowledge suffering.

This dynamic contributed to the frequent strife experienced by Sharon and Ed, a couple who sought my help. Sharon frequently complained that Ed was insensitive to much of her suffering, especially her migraine headaches. Ed, the oldest of three siblings, had a sister who had had child-hood cancer. As a child, he frequently helped with her care. While he did so lovingly, he also gradually grew to resent his sister, which shamed him. He came to recognize his sadness and distress over never receiving the attention he'd desired. By understanding his past, Ed became increasingly more sensitive to Sharon's pain.

Being compassionate to others can lead to great anxiety, frustration, or even feelings of helplessness. It can also trigger anger, especially when we try to ease their suffering and fail. This may make us believe we're inade-quate. The desire to avoid these highly unpleasant feelings leads many of us to minimize our compassion for others.

At times, you may feel overwhelmed by the pain you experience when being compassionate. It's helpful to remember that there's a difference between being empathetic and being compassionate. Compassion may start with empathy, but it moves beyond it, with caring, wisdom, and a wish to help reduce someone's anguish. This may mean simply sitting with a person in pain even when you can't fix it.

Your competitive desires compete with your desire to be compassionate. We live in a highly competitive society. All too often, it overemphasizes the im-portance of power, money, and possessions for happiness in life. When we make these goals our dominant priority, we can become so achievement-focused that we have little time or inclination for cultivating compassion. Being intensely competitive may interfere with our compassion toward professional rivals as well as our loved ones. We might seek to control or dominate others to fuel our egos. We may even conclude that being angry with our rivals is necessary if we are to maintain our edge.

Resolving this dilemma requires us to mindfully choose our priorities and the values we wish to live by. It involves determining how we can re-main compassionate with others while still striving to achieve our personal goals. We must remember that compassion for others and self-compassion are not mutually exclusive.

You believe that you need to eliminate your anger first. You may think you cannot be compassionate toward those who are the target of your anger. But cultivating compassion for others doesn't mean that you'll never get angry at them. Rather, it calls for you to be aware that you have a choice to be compassionate in every interaction.

Arousing Your Compassionate Self for Practicing Compassion to Others

Each of the exercises in this chapter calls for you to be mindfully and compassionately aware that we all suffer, desire safety, strive to achieve goals, and want to feel connected. This is the foundation for cultivating compassion for others, whether loving partners, family members, friends, coworkers, strangers you encounter throughout the day, or even people you may never meet.

Compassionate Meditations on Others

A powerful way to be habitually mindful of compassion in your relationships is to practice compassionate meditations on others. Buddhist scholar-practitioner Jeffrey Hopkins suggests that you first direct your compassion to friends or loved ones, then to neutral people—including those you may not know—and then to those who arouse your anger.[3] He recommends spending several weeks focusing on people in each category. Clearly, your greatest task may be focusing on those who make you angry. Try to identify your challenges and summon your mindfulness and self-compassion to help you move past them.

EXERCISE

Arousing Compassion for Others

Begin by engaging in mindfulness breathing for several moments. Then evoke your compassionate self, including the images, thoughts, emotions, and physical sensations that accompany it.

Now, envision the person to whom you want to direct your compassion.

1. Be mindful of this person's humanity.

2. Be mindful that this person desires safety, connection, and a fulfilling and happy life.

3. Be mindful that like all of us, this person has experienced suffering and challenges in life—perhaps some that may be especially painful and difficult to overcome.

4. Be mindful about remembering that this person has certain sensitivities to feeling threatened.

5. Be mindful about remembering that this person has accumulated a lifetime of habits, many of which he or she may be unaware of.

6. Be mindful of the truthfulness of these thoughts, regardless of how this person behaves.

Now, still envisioning the person and making this image as real as possible, simply think words of compassion such as the following:[4]

May you be safe.

May your life be peaceful.

May you be healthy.

May you be free of suffering.

As before, be mindful about any thoughts that compete for your attention while practicing this exercise. Be especially mindful of those obstacles, outlined above, that can interfere with your compassion. And again, use mindfulness as well as compassionate wisdom to accept and move past these obstacles.

While taking a bus to my office, I periodically choose one passenger to whom I'll direct compassion. I conjure up the circumstances of that person's life, the joys he or she may have experienced, and the suffering he or she may have endured. I certainly have no way of knowing the truth, but whenever I do this, I leave the bus with a feeling of warmth and calmness. Evoking my compassionate self in this way keeps me mindful of the overriding truth: each of us goes about our day with some personal mission in mind, and we're always influenced by our past when dealing with life's challenges. You may want to summon a similar moment of compassion while taking public transportation, waiting in line at the store, or stuck in the middle of traffic.

EXERCISE

Visualizing Others as Children

Most of us have fewer expectations of children than we do of adults. As such, it's sometimes easier to be compassionate to children who suffer than to adults. We may be more empathetic about their difficulties in problem solving, as well as their inability to fully take care of themselves. Consequently, it may be easier for us to show compassion for others when we view them as children.

Visualize the person as the child he or she once was and the child who has very strongly influenced the person he or she has become. This practice can be used in a general way or when you're trying to manage your anger. It's a positive practice that's not intended to belittle others but rather to evoke your caring and concern, to see beyond this person's behavior and to be mindful of the sources of his or her suffering or anger. It highlights the fact that child logic influences all of us.

Overcoming a Critical Mind

Be mindful of any tendency you have to criticize others in your thoughts, for their behavior, their appearance, or their simply being different from you. Be especially mindful during moments of anger arousal. Critical thoughts can powerfully undermine your ability to remember that this other person may also be suffering.

Such criticism, like destructive anger, is often just another form of self-compassion gone awry. It's often practiced in an effort to help us feel that we're better than others. Being critical may provide, if only for a moment, a rise in our sense of self-worth. But there's a cost. Such criticism only distracts us from recognizing our own imperfections, flaws, and weaknesses—in essence, our shared humanity. It's ironic that we're often the most critical of others when we feel that we're not a part of the larger humanity.

You may be critical of others if you're threatened by their differences. At such times, you may focus on a person's looks, behaviors, attitudes, ethnicity, or race. When this occurs, be mindful of your choices. When embracing compassion, you choose to focus on your similarities, regardless of the other person's culture or physical appearance.

EXERCISE

Recognizing Challenges to Being Compassionate to Others

Cultivating compassion for others involves being mindful when having critical thoughts about them. Answering the following questions may help you evoke your compassionate self:

1. Do I feel threatened by this person with regard to what I'm being critical about? If so, in what ways do I feel threatened?

2. Am I critical of traits or qualities that I have within myself and don't like or accept?

3. Am I critical of traits or qualities that I wouldn't like to see in myself?

4. What mindless habits may be contributing to my tendency to be critical?

5. What challenges to being compassionate may be contributing to my being critical?

6. What is the advantage of being critical of others?

Evoking the Framework for Anger as a Foundation for Compassion to Others

Just as you can use the framework for anger to promote self-awareness and self-compassion, it can serve as the foundation for furthering your compassion for others. Remind yourself that everyone you encounter is influenced by desires, thoughts, feelings, and physical sensations that are a part of their internal experiences. They have certain drives and expectations that move them. When feeling threatened, they may quickly form knee-jerk appraisals of others and of the world around them. And, like you, they also suffer.

Be mindful to speculate about the desires other people may have, especially those you may share. It's understandable that their behavior may capture your attention. This is especially true when you evoke compassion toward someone with whom you experience anger.

Cultivate compassion for their child logic. Regardless of our successes, intelligence, or age, we all behave at times like the child in the elementary school yard, the middle school cafeteria, or the high school classroom. We're often driven by those same powerful emotions that influenced us in our early years. This shows the power of child logic, especially when we feel threatened. Remember this, especially when you conclude that a person's beliefs or actions make no sense.

Cultivate compassion for their desires and expectations. Being mindful of our desires and expectations is important to understanding our anger, but it's especially important to remind ourselves that others' desires and expectations may differ from ours. This may sound simple and clear at first, but it's particularly challenging to remember this when we're being critical or judgmental.

Cultivate compassion for their appraisals and negative feelings, including anger. Being compassionate toward others means remembering that, like you, they form appraisals and experience negative feelings that may influence their actions. This may include being sensitive to their hot buttons. Remember that they may want to protect themselves in their particular areas of vulnerability. Self-compassion can help you understand your own vulnerabilities, and cultivating compassion for others will help you become mindful of the vulnerabilities in others that they see as weaknesses and flaws.

Empathy and Sympathy: Key Attributes in Cultivating Compassion for Others

Cultivating compassion for others calls for improving our ability to practice empathy and sympathy.

Empathy

Just as developing empathy for ourselves helps us recognize our own humanity, empathy for others is key to recognizing their humanity. It calls for identifying with the feelings of others and pondering what has contributed to their thinking and behaviors. It reflects mindful attention that moves us beyond our own perspectives. Empathy is what helps us form connections with those we love, our neighbors, and our friends. It also allows us to momentarily identify with characters in books, movies, and songs. And, it's empathy that keeps us emotionally invested in them even when they're vastly different from ourselves. It's notable that some of the best movies and novels can move an audience or readers to empathize with even the most heinous villains.

The more resilient you are in sitting with your own feelings, the more empathetic you can be with others. The more you work at being empathetic, the more rapidly you'll humanize others, even when you're angry with them. This practice can help you feel less vulnerable to feeling threatened and less prone to destructive anger.

Expanding Your Empathy for Others

Take some time to practice the following exercise with your significant other, friends, family members, coworkers, and neighbors. Evoke your compassionate self as you envision each of these individuals. One at a time, direct your empathy toward them, using the following guidelines:

1. Observe the person's behavior, including facial expression and posture.

2. Notice the content and tone of his or her conversation.

3. Are this person's facial expressions consistent with the conversation? Is his or her behavior consistent with what's being said?

4. How do your observations influence how you feel toward this person?

5. Based on your knowledge of this person, what do your observations tell you about his or her feelings?

6. Now, identify any feelings that may be very different from those you initially believed this person to be experiencing.

7. Remind yourself: be mindful that this person's actions make sense when his or her past experiences are considered.

Expanding Empathy by Understanding Others' Backstory

From the time I was a child growing up in New York City, I was always curious about people. I wanted to know more about their character and the experiences that had led to their being the person they had become. I spent a great deal of time observing people, whether traveling on the subway or visiting Jones Beach on a hot summer day. Clearly, this curiosity was just a precursor to what I'd later choose as my life's work.

Though you may not make a career of it, being mindful of the lives of others can greatly expand your capacity for empathy. Just as when watching movies or plays or reading novels, you need to know the backstory to understand why others behave the way they do. This can help you identify factors that have shaped their personalities, led to their desires and expectations, and influenced their feelings and behaviors.

This type of mindfulness helps all of us to see the humanity in others. We look beyond what's immediately observable. A major component of letting go of anger is to curiously explore what leads a person to be the way he or she is. This reinforces the concept that how a person thinks, feels, and behaves makes sense given his or her past experiences. Through this lens, we can clearly see that while most of us share the same desires to be free of suffering, to feel safe, and to have happiness, we may address these desires in very different ways. Searching for the details of people's past powerfully contributes to seeing them in a more compassionate light.

Answering questions like those in the next exercise can help you achieve this by generating guesses about what others are experiencing. Your answers can help you better understand what shapes their current behavior.

EXERCISE

Questions to Help You Understand Others

First, answer the following questions about someone you feel positive toward, then about someone you feel neutral toward, and finally, about someone with whom you experience conflict and anger.

1. What desires seem to underlie this person's behavior and attitudes? (Review those listed in chapter 7 for further ideas.)

2. What might this person's expectations be, especially those influenced by child logic?

3. What appraisals might this person form that depend on his or her current situation in life or a specific interaction you've recently shared?

4. Pretend for a moment that you're creating a film or writing a book about this person. Identify or make up details about his or her past that you might include to help the audience become more empathetic with and sympathetic toward this character.

5. Do you notice any shift in your mind and body as you mindfully answer these questions?

6. How might your understanding affect your relating to this person if you wanted to decrease his or her suffering?

7. Identify those behaviors or attitudes that you disagree with the most. Now, identify a past that might help you empathize with an individual who exhibits these behaviors or attitudes.

Embracing Sympathy

Just as self-compassion involves being moved by your own pain, sympathy is about being moved by the suffering of others. Sympathy may involve sadness about their pain, which can fuel your need to ease their suffering. And, just as you may face obstacles to being empathetic, you may experience challenges to being sympathetic. Being open to sympathy allows us to act with compassion. Again, it requires that you don't deny, minimize, or rationalize your own pain.

During a session, one of my clients, Jason, told me he'd passed by a homeless person the previous day. The man was sitting on the sidewalk with his arm outstretched, holding a paper cup. This is a very familiar sight to anyone living in a large city. Jason said that in the past, he would turn his face away. He realized that his knee-jerk reaction was to think, "Yeah, sure. He'll only go and spend it on liquor." This was a message Jason had heard many times. He'd also recognized that his attitude came in part from his father's alcohol abuse. Jason has now changed. He often donates in these situations. He said that when friends ask him why he so often gives money or food to panhandlers, he says with satisfaction, "It makes me feel good and I can afford to."

This anecdote demonstrates Jason's shift in attitude, then in behavior. He realized that he had many opportunities each day to show compassion in his thoughts, feelings, and actions.

* * *

This chapter has focused on helping you *think* and *feel* more compassionately toward others. In the next chapter, you'll find practices that can help you *behave* with compassion toward others.

For Further Reflection

1. What do you believe are your most powerful challenges to showing compassion to others?

2. Did the people who took care of you as a child share any thoughts or attitudes about compassion toward others? Try to identify those expressed by parents, relatives, friends, neighbors, teachers, the community, your religion, and any others that may have influenced you.

3. Compassion for others and self-compassion go hand in hand. If you've been practicing the strategies in this book, this might be a good time to once again complete the Self-Compassion Inventory that Kristin Neff provides at http://selfcompassion.org.

4. Use the model of anger to make sense of others' anger, especially the negative emotions that trigger it. Try to identify what you believe they may be experiencing. What could they have done to counter their destructive anger?

5. For one week, be mindful of your critical thoughts about others as you go about your day. Mindfully meditate on identifying why you're critical. Think about whether your criticism distracts you from addressing issues about yourself.

6. The following week, commit not only to being mindful of your critical thoughts but also to forming compassionate thoughts instead.

CHAPTER 13

Self-Compassionate and Compassionate Interactions with Others

It's one thing to intend to be compassionate and another to actually behave that way. Mindfulness meditations on compassion toward others contribute powerfully to compassion in our thoughts, but being mindful to *behave* compassionately is more meaningful. Both attitudes and actions can show self-compassion, lending us a deep sense of connection and safety as we help others. Compassion is essential to practicing healthy anger. As you read this chapter, think about what encourages and supports your compassion toward others.

Assertive Communication

Communicating assertively means acknowledging our needs and desires, telling others how their behavior has affected us, and requesting action. It allows others to understand us better. Whether used with loved ones, friends, coworkers, or people we encounter in our daily lives, assertive communication demonstrates both self-compassion and compassion at the same time. Assertiveness supports the practice of healthy anger.

Assertive communication requires you to be mindful of your needs, desires, and feelings. You must connect with yourself in a meaningful way. Many of the practices you've learned so far have helped deepen the relationship you have with yourself. The practices in this chapter will help you become more authentic and connected in your relationships with others.

Preparing for Assertive Communication

Suppose you've thought about an episode of anger that you experienced with someone and have completed the Anger Log to understand it better. Suppose you've identified the thoughts and feelings you'd like to address. You'll find it enlightening to answer these questions before sharing your concerns with the person:

1. *What are the benefits of sharing my thoughts and feelings?* It may not always be necessary or beneficial. For example, you may decide to share these thoughts and feelings with those closest to you but not with your casual friends. Or, after pondering the situation, you may conclude there's little need to share them at all.

2. *What do I hope to achieve in my communication?* You may hope that, in the future, others will be more mindful of how their behaviors affect you. Or, you may simply want to show your true self in a more intimate relationship. Be attentive to when your reason for sharing is really to minimize or even deny your own blame for the matter.

3. *What can I expect from being assertive?* Be mindful to distinguish between what you hope to achieve and what you expect to achieve. Unrealistic expectations may only make you angrier. Be honest with yourself when you're sharing so as to persuade someone to change his or her behavior. There may be times, though, when you expect little change but feel empowered through your assertiveness.

4. *Have I selected the best moment to express myself?* The ideal time for your discussion is after you have sufficiently calmed yourself. And you increase the chances of your message being heard when the other person is calm enough to genuinely hear it.

The Assertiveness Model

The assertiveness model that follows is perhaps the most candid and least threatening way to show another person our thoughts and feelings.[1] Assertive communication displays a level of intimacy that can further a discussion about our desires in a relationship. Please note that while sharing both feelings and thoughts may be very useful in personal relationships, baring your feelings at work may not be appropriate (I elaborate on this later in the chapter). The following guidelines are helpful for communicating assertively about your anger.

1. *Begin the conversation with a positive statement.* Begin with a statement that's sincere and relevant—one that highlights a positive aspect of your relationship. Ideally, refer to the specific conflict.

   Example: "I really enjoy and value the time we share together, whether going to a restaurant, to a concert, or just spending time at home."

2. *Address a specific observable behavior.* The second statement identifies the feelings you experienced in reaction to someone's behavior. This isn't a judgment but rather a clear statement about how the person's behavior affected you. Point out a specific and observable behavior rather than focus on the person as a whole. Share the key negative feelings that preceded your anger: "When you [specific observable behavior], I feel [the negative feelings that precede your anger]."

   Example: "When you *frequently cancel our plans at the last minute*, I feel *disappointed and disrespected*."

3. *Share your negative feeling as it arouses anger.* "And when I feel [the negative feelings that precede your anger], I become [angry, annoyed, or irritated, etc.]." This sentence offers insight into the source of your anger. Be thoughtful here. Some people may view the word *anger* as threatening and associate it with aggression or abandonment. At first, you may want to simply say that you're "intensely annoyed" or "intensely irritated." Then gradually use the word *anger* as you emphasize—and they realize—that it's just a feeling.

   Example: "When I felt *disappointed and disrespected*, I started to feel *annoyed*."

4. *Identify what you, ideally, would like to happen next time.* This final statement is a request. As such, it's least likely to arouse a sense of threat. It may merely serve as a point for negotiation. "Next time, I would greatly appreciate it if you would [a preferred behavior] instead."

   Example: "Next time, I would greatly appreciate it if you would *let me know sooner if you can't make it* instead."

At times, the person you're communicating with may immediately agree to your request. He or she may feel encouraged to pay more attention to your desires in the future. Even assertive communication, however, is no guarantee that you'll get what you want. Your message may not be well received in spite of your best efforts. Some people are highly sensitive to the slightest mention of negative feelings and will think you're attacking their self-worth. Or, they may feel threatened if they view your feedback as rejection, betrayal, or even emotional abandonment.

People who feel toxic shame or guilt or think only in black and white may grow furious in response to your comments. If this happens, state your positive feelings again. Emphasize that your feelings are reactions to very specific behaviors and not judgments of the person. Let them know that you're committed to improving the relationship and that you don't intend to devalue them in any way.

It's possible that the person will respond with an angry comment such as, "I really don't care what you feel!" You may want to try being assertive at another time if he or she is really too enraged to listen. But, if the person typically responds this way whenever you mention your feelings and desires, you may need to realize that your relationship has more serious troubles than simply communication. This situation calls for further self-reflection and perhaps support from a counselor.

The Differences between Assertive, Aggressive, and Passive Communication

Here are some guidelines for distinguishing assertive communication from aggressive or passive ways of communicating.

Assertive communication

- expresses your internal experience as a result of being mindful about how an event affected you;
- requests to talk about the issue instead of trying to blame or shame the person who has contributed to your pain; and
- demonstrates your attempt to begin a discussion rather than to stifle or end it.

Aggressive communication

- may involve a power play, emphasizing that you're right and that the person you're addressing is wrong;

- may judge and devalue the person as a whole rather than focus on his or her behavior;

- may belittle a person's intelligence, skills, common sense, or other personal attributes;

- may convey disrespect, violate the person's rights, and heighten his or her feelings of threat; and

- may shut down communication, as a defensive reaction to anger.

Unassertive or passive communication

- lacks self-compassion;

- involves being dishonest when expressing thoughts or feelings;

- makes you feel invisible in a relationship and ultimately, more prone to anger;

- causes you to minimize or deny the importance of your desires, feelings, or thoughts; and

- leads others to view you as easygoing and flexible, with no needs or desires worth mentioning.

Being assertive means being authentic. It's essential for healthy anger in all relationships and is especially relevant in our most intimate relationships.

Practicing Mindfulness and Compassion in Your Most Intimate Relationship

When two people form a romantic relationship, they bring unique personalities and pasts to their bond. And each person's past has shaped that individual's ideas about how a loved one should respond to his or her needs, desires, and expectations. Most relevant to this chapter, people also keep their old habits, including the way they manage anger when a partner appears to threaten or ignore these needs, desires, and expectations. It's not surprising that even the most loving relationships occasionally involve conflict and anger. And when one or both partners are prone to anger, these conflicts can cause tremendous discord.

Agreeing to Terms of Engagement

Practicing mindfulness and compassion throughout a relationship helps a couple feel safe and connected with each other, even during moments of tension. Agreeing in advance about how to approach each other during episodes of anger shows each partner's commitment.

As a beginning point, remember that the worst time to argue is when you're furiously angry. As shown throughout this book, this is when you're most likely to mindlessly succumb to your old habits of destructive anger. During these moments, you may focus on your own grievances without genuinely hearing your partner's. The following guidelines offer a clear approach to dealing with conflict—one that's rooted in mindfulness, self-compassion, and compassion for your partner. I encourage you to discuss these guidelines with your partner and sign a pledge showing your commitment to follow them.

1. *We commit to practicing healthy anger.* Healthy anger is the basis for constructively managing conflicts and anger within your relationship. One person may struggle with destructive anger. It's to your mutual benefit as a couple to learn and practice mindfulness, self-compassion, and compassion as presented in this book.

2. *We will discuss our differences only when we are sufficiently calm, and we agree to cease the discussion if either of us feels too agitated or threatened.* Be mindful of your own level of comfort, whether you're agitated or calm. Agree in advance to immediately stop the discussion if either person feels a discomfort level of 4, based on 1 being comfortable and 10 being intensely uncomfortable. Be mindful of any urge you may have to have the last word, believing that, by doing so, you and your partner will finally reach a truce. Also, be mindful that your partner might feel anxious about ending the discussion while knowing you're still angry. Discuss this in advance.

3. *We agree to a word or phrase to signal that either of us needs to disengage and cease further discussion.* Agree in advance to a word that either person can say to immediately stop the discussion. Speaking the word means that too much tension exists to constructively continue. Select a word that's lighthearted or whimsical, as a way to provide some levity when things are heating up. One couple I

worked with used the word *avalanche*. They were both skiers and knew about the hazardous consequences of loud noises on the slopes. Another couple used the words *puppy's feet*. Each was a dog lover who readily shared a pleasant childhood memory about a puppy. Another couple chose *turtle* to convey a need to retreat. They purchased two stuffed toy turtles and placed one in the living room and the other in the kitchen. Rather than saying the word, either would hold up the toy as a signal to end the discussion.

4. *Ideally, we will resume the activity we had planned prior to having the conflict. Or, we may instead need solitude.* Some people are able to engage in an activity together, such as watching a movie or going out for dinner, immediately after agreeing to shelve a discussion. Others need solitude. If this is the case, I strongly recommend that you go to a different room rather than leave the house. Leaving home at that moment might trigger further anxiety for a partner, especially if he or she is sensitive to abandonment issues. It sends a message that you might take flight whenever things become too heated. Furthermore, leaving the house in a fit of anger can trigger hot buttons regarding trust.

5. *If we decide to stop a discussion without a resolution, we will resume the discussion at another time when both of us are sufficiently calm.* You may decide to resume your discussion an hour later or even several days later. But both parties need to commit to solving the issue. If your anger escalates during the next attempt, stop, calm down, and try again at a later time. Unresolved conflicts will most likely surface again. And while they may not be about the same issue, they'll most likely reflect some underlying tension that you haven't yet addressed. Failing to discuss the identified issue only undermines this entire agreement.

6. *We will be mindful of time limits.* All too often, couples tell me that their arguments last into the night. You may find that when an argument begins at eight o'clock at night, you continue it for several hours. Begin the same argument at eight o'clock in the morning, when one or both of you have to leave for work, and you're more likely to end the conflict. I recommend thirty to forty minutes as the limit for such discussions. If you have little resolution during

this time, you may want to temporarily agree to disagree and resume your discussion later. Consider alternative ways of expressing your desires when you do so.

7. *We will not argue in the bedroom.* Avoid arguing in the bedroom—especially late at night, just before going to bed. It can lead you to associate the heightened tension of anger with sleep or physical intimacy. Your emotional mind is more reactive, especially when you're tired. You'll most likely forget what you said by morning, and staying up late will only leave you irritable the next day. In fact, a recent study suggests that when just one partner doesn't get enough sleep, couples are more likely to experience conflicts and empathize less with each other.[2] Years ago, some psychotherapists said that couples should never go to bed angry. This is certainly an ideal that both of you can aspire to. However, there's a huge difference between agreeing to disagree and becoming so enraged that one of you leaves the argument and withdraws.

How to Respond during Moments of Anger Arousal with Your Partner

The moment when your anger with your partner is aroused calls for you to evoke all the practices you've learned so far for self-compassion and compassion. The following guidelines offer further direction:

1. *Stop, and calm your body.* Cease whatever you're doing and evoke your compassionate self in order to sit with your physical and emotional tension. Engage in deep breathing and mindfulness breathing and relax your mind and body as best you can. Decreasing your tendency to destructive anger depends on your ability to regain composure after a triggering event.

2. *Arouse compassion and self-compassion.* Become mindful of what is going on right now. It's the moment of encounter, when you and your partner feel some form of emotional pain and threat. You can choose to focus on recognizing and understanding that threat or solely on your anger.

3. *Be mindful of your needs and desires and those of your partner.* Your anger is a cue that some needs or desires are threatened. Try to identify them. Similarly, practice compassion as you guess which

of your partner's desires are threatened. Refer to the framework for anger to better understand both yourself and your partner.

4. *Be mindful of and compassionate toward the thoughts and negative feelings that lead you to experience anger.* Be compassionate to what your partner may be experiencing. Be mindful of those feelings that underlie your anger, whether or not you actually share them at this moment. While evoking your compassionate self, try to understand your partner's hurts and experiences with the same curiosity and openness that you show toward your own. This is a moment when you can choose to be empathetic and sensitive to your partner's suffering.

5. *Be mindful of and compassionate toward your expectations and appraisals and those of your partner.* Identify and evaluate your expectations and appraisals. Consider other perspectives that may decrease your anger. Be especially mindful to recognize an unrealistic expectation or a knee-jerk appraisal. Evoke your compassionate wisdom to help you recognize your partner's expectations and appraisals.

6. *Speak slowly and lower your voice.* It takes practice, but speaking in a slow, low tone is a powerful approach to achieving calmness. Remember, emotions are contagious. Acting out your anger may only intensify your partner's feelings of threat, whereas your calmness can help lessen them.

7. *Practice visualization.* Engage your compassionate self to visualize the hurting part of your partner from his or her past or present. This will further your mindfulness to be compassionate and to acknowledge that child logic may be playing a major role in how your partner is reacting.

How to Help Defuse Your Partner's Anger during Conflict and Anger Arousal

These guidelines are intended to help you defuse your partner's anger during conflicts. They support the guidelines provided above.

1. *Promote eye contact.* It's much easier to remain angry when yelling across the room or even through the entire house. When you are calm, direct eye contact promotes increased feelings of

connection. It also arouses compassion. It's a nonverbal way to communicate, "Look at me. I'm the same person who loves you even though I'm angry with you."

2. *Sit down in a comfortable chair.* Standing can increase your agitation. Sitting can help you relax. Suggest that you and your partner sit on the most comfortable sofa or chairs in your home.

3. *Compassionately acknowledge your partner's anger and negative feelings.* Suppose you simply say, "I can tell you're angry." This provides validation. And although recognizing the feelings behind your partner's anger shows compassion, it's best to guess them rather than state them as fact. For example, you might say, "I really can't read your mind, but maybe you're feeling hurt, ignored, or disappointed. Can we talk about that?"

4. *Remain silent and listen.* Anger requires energy. It's often only ten to fifteen minutes before your partner tires and slows down. If you can remain calm, being silent and listening may help defuse his or her anger. Genuinely hear your partner so you can clearly recognize the internal experiences that led to the anger. Communicate that you're listening both with your words and through your facial expressions and body language. And be sure to pay careful attention to your partner's experience as a whole, not just a word or phrase.

5. *Partially agree.* Finding agreement is a major tenet of any successful negotiation. You and your partner will both feel empowered when you agree in some ways rather than just differ. Agreement helps foster connection, promotes empathy, and diminishes threat.

   Accusations that you "always" or "never" do something make it especially challenging to agree on anything. Such statements are global and more easily viewed as criticisms of the person rather than of his or her behavior. This may only heighten your partner's vulnerability to anger.

   Agreeing in part is one way to respond under such circumstances. Suppose that your partner says, "You are so stupid." You might respond with, "Sometimes I do stupid things." Or, your partner proclaims, "You never remember what I say!" You might say, "I can be forgetful at times."

This isn't necessarily the time to address your partner's tendency to think globally. However, it can be constructive to share this observation at a later time when you're discussing your relationship in general rather than trying to solve an issue.

6. *Admit your contribution to the situation.* Being able to admit that you contributed to the conflict, whether by jumping to conclusions or having unrealistic expectations, shows your willingness to communicate. This will help move you toward candid discussion and reduce your tendency to attack or go on the defensive.

7. *Freeze-focus, or defer from reviewing the past at this moment.* A *freeze-focus response* is one that you repeat in an effort to focus on the current concern. For example, your partner may tell you, "Last month you did the same thing when we went to dinner with Raul and Marie. And in June . . . remember? You also kept me waiting for an hour when we planned to see a show!"

A freeze-focus response might be, "Clearly, you still have feelings about those other incidents and we need to discuss them. I can only handle one thing at a time. Could we only discuss what just happened?" You may be confused, if not frustrated, by your partner's bringing up the past. However, this clearly indicates that he or she harbors unresolved feelings about it. If this occurs, remind yourself that your partner may be feeling vulnerable to threatening feelings. He or she may be holding on to the past in an effort at self-protection. Listen to whatever your partner says and remember to bring it up in a future conversation.

8. *Set limits.* Setting limits is something you do for yourself. It reflects self-compassion and compassion. Maybe you are becoming too agitated or feel threatened, despite attempts by both of you to defuse the situation.

Setting limits may entail saying your special word or phrase to end the conversation, as part of your terms of engagement. Or, you might say, "I can tell you're angry and hurt and I'm open to discussing how you're feeling. But I don't deserve to be yelled or cursed at." Or, "I can tell you're upset, but it's me. While you may feel the need to continue, I don't believe anything I say right now is going to be constructive."

Withdrawal is another approach to setting limits, especially if you feel threatened. Assertively state your reason for doing so, and then withdraw. Let your partner know that you want to discuss the issue at another time but that you don't feel comfortable doing so at the present time.

9. *Seek assistance when you feel physically threatened.* Practicing self-compassion means doing what is wise and in your best interest. Being mindful of your physical safety should be a priority. Listen to your wisdom during angry interactions if it tells you to leave and find help.

You may learn a lot about your partner and your relationship if these strategies don't work. For example, your partner may have difficulty calming and refuse to end the discussion. If this occurs, try to identify what he or she may be experiencing. Letting go of anger may not be the issue. Your partner may feel intensely threatened and anxious over your disappointment and anger. Provide reassurance that you care. Indicate that even though you're working on anger management, you aren't going to be sufficiently clear-minded to discuss the issue any further. You might ask your partner to identify what you can do to help him or her become calm.

Remember that you can only control how *you* behave. You can try to persuade, cajole, or negotiate to defuse your partner's anger, but at some point you may need to realize that you can't control your partner.

These strategies may also fail when your partner clings to anger for all of the reasons described in earlier chapters. If this seems to be the issue, you might ask, "What is it I can say or do that can help you with your anger?" The answer can be very informative and revealing. Even when you're being truly sensitive and compassionate, your partner may have difficulty identifying what you can do to help. He or she may need to determine what needs to happen to let go of his or her anger. Assure your partner that you intend to forget the past and make a change—one for the better. Be mindful that your partner is ultimately responsible for identifying what he or she needs in order to let go of anger.

Sharing Your Completed Anger Logs to Foster Mutual Compassion

Sharing a completed Anger Log can be very effective at furthering communication, understanding, and compassion with each other. It calls for a high level of comfort and trust.

Begin by telling your partner about the strategies you've learned for more effectively practicing healthy anger. Ideally, encourage your partner to read this book. Then, suggest that each of you complete an Anger Log on a conflict you've recently had with each other. Take turns to share your completed logs.

I've found this extremely helpful for developing compassion, especially with couples that are truly committed to working on anger management together. Reviewing each other's Anger Log can be both revealing and surprising. Each partner gains increased insight into the other's pain. Such sharing promotes further understanding, which supports mutual compassion. Often, each partner is surprised at the other's expectations. It may be the first time they've heard these expectations. When examined out loud, some are clearly unrealistic. On other occasions, partners fail to recognize each other's appraisals and must admit that they were well off target when guessing them.

Using this approach, you'll become sensitized to the needs and desires that drive your own and your partner's anger. Sharing your most meaningful desires reflects true intimacy. You and your partner will discover each other's uniqueness. Sharing responses to the Anger Log will expand your mindfulness of and compassion for each other's differences—as well as the similarities that might bring you closer.

Being out of sync with each other's expectations and failing to recognize each other's needs and desires lead to conflict and disappointment. Differences in these areas can very quickly lead to threatening feelings. But they also offer opportunities for negotiation and compromise. And in some situations, differences may lead to sadness rather than anger when they are seen as unresolvable.

As repeatedly emphasized in this chapter, solving these conflicts calls for increased mindfulness to be compassionate with your partner. Expand your repertoire for doing so, even when it may not come naturally at first.

Being Mindful about Expanding the Positive

Strengthening your connection with your partner is vital for reducing his or her feelings of threat. It requires you to be mindful. In her powerfully enlightening book *Love 2.0*, psychologist Barbara Frederickson discusses the concept of *positivity resonance*. This is what we experience when we form loving connections with others.[3] She states that such love is a moment of connection that includes the sharing of positive emotions, attuned responses at the most basic mind and body level, and mutual care. She suggests that our most loving relationships involve many such moments.

According to John Gottman, one of the most recognized authorities on relationships, it's the building and maintaining of such a connection that determines the stability of a relationship.[4] He recommends that couples do the following for a lasting and thriving relationship:

1. Get to know each other: each other's driving forces, dreams, likes, dislikes, etc.

2. Be mindful of each other's positive qualities and of positive feelings for each other.

3. Interact frequently to share thoughts and experiences.

4. Share in making decisions.

5. Communicate assertively.

6. Look beyond behavior and try to understand how feeling and thinking may prevent agreement.

7. Expand what you share: values, traditions, goals, and interests.

Forming a genuine connection and helping to reduce threat in your relationship require a commitment to be mindful and compassionate.

Practicing Compassion in the Workplace

Practicing compassion in the work setting has its unique challenges. Work typically demands that we be task-focused. All too often, this competes with being sensitive to how people feel. Additionally, many factors in the workplace can potentially trigger feelings of threat and anger. These include

- concerns about fairness and recognition;
- concerns about job and financial security;
- encouragement and rewards for intense competition;
- demands for productivity;
- deadlines; and
- long hours.

It's understandable that we may have difficulty viewing those we work with as individuals with desires, thoughts, and feelings. It may also be challenging to look beyond their behavior. In his best-selling book *Social Intelligence*, Daniel Goleman says that being aware of others' feelings is essential for emotional intelligence and is highly valuable in the workplace.[5] Empathy and sympathy can help foster good relationships in the work setting, regardless of the circumstances or the position one holds. Practicing compassion with our coworkers means being sensitive to their safety needs, their motivations at work, and their desires for connection. Compassion can pave the way for people to attain shared goals. This leads to increased productivity, whether in the context of teamwork, supervision, negotiations, or brainstorming.

Here are some strategies that can help you cultivate compassion in the workplace:

1. *Understand your anger and that of others in terms of the framework for anger.* Complete an Anger Log on incidents at work that arouse anger. This will help you become aware of what you expect from your work setting. Be especially mindful of mixed or conflicting expectations. These may undermine your focus or that of your supervisor, coworkers, or those you supervise.

2. *Practice the assertiveness model in communication, but without emphasizing feelings.* Sharing feelings is essential in a personal relationship, but at work, it may be more constructive to discuss your expectations and appraisals. Suppose your supervisor is two months late completing your six-month evaluation. This evaluation was promised as part of your contract, and you've become increasingly irritated at his failure to complete it. You'd certainly be concerned, knowing full well that such an evaluation can affect job security, a potential raise, and maybe even enrollment in a pension program. So you may be intensely disappointed, anxious, and angry. Rather than discussing your anger, however, it would be far more constructive to say, "I was expecting an evaluation a while ago. I'm not sure what I should conclude." And, if your supervisor answers, "Oh. Sorry about that. I'll get back to you," you can respond with, "When might I expect that?"

3. *When you are angry with others, address how their specific behaviors affect productivity in the workplace or with the team.* Suppose you become annoyed when a member of your department arrives late. Rather than making it personal, you might instead say, "When you come in late, others have to drop what they are doing to cover for you." Other examples include: "I believe what you said shut down our brainstorming ideas for the project." Or, "When you said that in the meeting, you hurt the coworkers' morale."

4. *Be aware that certain language may arouse irritation.* Avoid telling others they "have to" or "must" do something, especially in anger. Rather, share your expectations. Then inquire whether they are willing to meet them. When indicated, share the possible consequences if they aren't able to do so.

5. *Be mindful of how realistic your expectations are in your workplace.* We bring many expectations based on our desires to the workplace. Some may have to do with financial or emotional security or the opportunity for challenge or creativity. We may harbor expectations about how the company, boss, or coworkers should treat us. Be mindful that some expectations may be satisfied, some may be challenged, and others may never be met.

   You may never obtain that promotion you hoped for, even when you've excelled in your work. Unfortunately, other factors may be involved in the decision—some that you may believe are totally irrelevant. Or, your desire for stability may be severely challenged when your company unexpectedly announces plans to merge with another. You might be disappointed if you desire greater social connection but your workplace culture doesn't support it.

   Remembering that you have a choice is a powerful way to avoid feeling victimized, a key contributor to anger arousal. Focus on the reasons you keep working where you do. This isn't to deny or minimize your complaints but to highlight what's positive about your situation. Contemplating what you appreciate about your job is one way to look at the big picture. Of course, when your grievances outweigh the advantages, you may decide you need to move on.

   The workplace has undergone significant changes in recent years. It's important to be resilient when it comes to your expectations. Self-compassion and compassion for others are fundamental to such resilience.

6. *Try to identify expectations and appraisals about your workplace that are similar to those you have had in your personal life.* Be mindful of habits in your closest relationships that may surface at the workplace. These may include feelings about competition or authority, past hurts or distrust, sibling rivalry, or attitudes toward men and women in general. The workplace is often the ground on which these are played out. This is understandable given that you might spend your entire day, every day, interacting with the same group of people.

   Be mindful that you may be reminded, consciously or without full awareness, of people from your past. Such reminders may be good or bad, depending on those previous relationships. Similarly, be mindful of expectations that echo experiences from your childhood or family life. These can leave you vulnerable to certain hot buttons.

   Work can challenge your capacity to practice self-compassion and compassion for others. But practicing both is essential for healthy anger and a productive workplace.

7. *Practice compassionate meditations on those with whom you work.* Personal desires, expectations, feelings, and the need for connection and safety, well-being, and happiness don't cease during work hours. Try to be mindful of this throughout the day. Practice mindfulness meditations on your coworkers and be mindful to engage in everyday interactions that show compassion.

Acting with Self-Compassion and Compassion When in Conflict

Many of our interactions can leave us feeling threatened if we're prone to anger. More often than not, this may occur simply because others behave in ways that don't satisfy our expectations. *Conflict,* by definition, is a process in which one party perceives that his or her interests are being opposed or negatively affected by another party. For example, perhaps you hold a certain view about parenting, one that's more authoritarian than your spouse's. Or, you may find yourself arguing with a friend over sports, religion, or politics, or with a neighbor about the height of a shrub that divides your yards. You may experience conflict with coworkers or those you encounter going about your day, such as a cashier, waiter, delivery person, or grocer.

These encounters give you the chance to mindfully practice compassion. You have the opportunity to view people's behaviors and attitudes against the backdrop of their desires—as well as their potential to feel threat.

Practicing compassion toward others requires us to remain mindful, especially during moments of conflict. It may involve compromise and giving priority to what's really important to us in the big picture. The following suggestions offer some advice.

Admit When You Are Wrong

We become less vulnerable to feeling threatened when we're free to acknowledge our mistakes or weaknesses. Self-compassion enables us to do so.

Apologizing decreases the sense of threat in others. Apologizing encompasses both self-compassion and compassion. One of my class participants demonstrated this when he admitted to his neighbor that he had misunderstood what she'd said. Another took responsibility for causing a fender-bender, and another simply said, "You're right," when his friend criticized him.

Your challenge during conflicts is to evoke your compassionate self to manage your feelings and express yourself constructively. Also, focus on your shared humanity.

In his delightful book *Why Do I Love These People?* Po Bronson explores the many faces of family conflict and how they can be resolved.[6] He includes a story about a couple that divorced after the wife found out the husband was having an affair. The man was sincerely remorseful and despondent. Attempting to win her back, he sent letters, made phone calls, and bought her flowers. He was unable to rekindle her love. For an entire year, he mowed her lawn every week. He was relentless in demonstrating that he hadn't given up on their relationship and that he wasn't going anywhere. His determination paid off. Shortly after the one-year anniversary of their divorce, they married again. Compassion takes many forms.

Let Go of Power

Letting go of power is a compassionate way to reduce conflict, either in a loving relationship or during an encounter with a stranger. In fact, a study of hundreds of couples indicated that letting go of power was more important than just an apology.[7] The desired behaviors for letting go of power included, from most to least common:

- To show investment: show in words and actions the importance of resolving the conflict
- To stop adversarial behavior: be mindful of words, nonverbal behaviors, and actions that are aggressive or unkind
- To communicate more: keep talking
- To give affection
- To apologize

While giving affection may not be essential with a stranger, every one of these qualities shows how we can relate to others from our compassionate self during conflicts.

Drawing on your use of the anger framework, you might apologize by starting with how you were affected. Then, recognize the impact your behavior had on the person you're addressing. Some examples of this approach are saying:

I'm sorry for raising my voice. You're right. I guess I felt criticized. I wasn't thinking about what you needed at the time. I'll try to work on that more.

I apologize for being so critical about what you said. You don't deserve that. I'll try to be more sensitive when I give you feedback in the future.

I'm sorry for not picking you up first. I wasn't thinking of what you were feeling at the time. I'll try to listen better from now on.

A true apology involves accepting responsibility without blaming others. It entails trying to correct the situation and empathizing with the hurt, threat, or sense of neglect we've caused. We must state our intention to be more attentive the next time. And it also requires following through on our intentions, especially in ongoing relationships.

Give

Evoke your compassionate self to give compassionately. Savor the moment of giving, whether handing money to someone, writing a check to a charity, or paying a compliment. Be mindful to be fully present with both the satisfaction of giving and the recipient's appreciation. When you do offer personal compliments, comment on the person and his or her unique attributes rather than on appearance. You'll help others value themselves for who they are rather than how they look.

Giving information that you believe can be helpful to others is another form of compassion. Whether providing directions to a tourist, advising your child, helping your spouse, or interacting with coworkers, such giving allows you to experience both self-compassion and compassion.

Offer encouraging words to others. After all, you know how good it feels to receive them. Remember that, if possible, it's always more helpful to be an encourager than a discourager.

Forgiveness is also a form of giving, especially when you actually say it. When you accept an apology, you're helping to ease the other person's pain. Forgiveness involves many aspects of compassion and self-compassion in our thoughts and sometimes in our actions. As described in chapter 12, forgiveness may involve practicing forms of self-compassion that help you let go of resentment.

Be Mindful Not to Be Critical

The previous chapter suggested becoming mindful of the criticisms you form in your thoughts about others and yourself. It's to your advantage to better understand why you criticize. The following questions should help:

1. What purpose does it serve you to be critical?

2. Does being critical derive from your feeling threatened in some manner?

3. Is your criticism related to anger or simply disappointment and frustration that you haven't yet resolved?

4. Does being critical somehow help you feel empowered?

5. Are you inadvertently targeting someone with criticism because you're angry with someone else?

6. How might you reframe your comment or thought to avoid being judgmental?

7. How might you alter your nonverbal behavior—your tone, facial expression, or posture—to avoid appearing judgmental?

After considering your answers to these questions, you may resolve to cease being critical—or even to apologize.

Be Mindful of Everyday Opportunities to Practice Compassion

We have numerous opportunities to practice compassion with others every day. Doing so requires us to be mindful of whether we're task-focused, self-focused, or unfocused, which may interfere with being compassionate to others. I'm not suggesting we give up behaving in these modes but rather that we be mindful of when we're in them.

Acting with kindness toward others is a form of the deepest compassion. This may be expressed by helping a sick neighbor, volunteering for a cause that we value, providing assistance to those who are less fortunate than us, spearheading political action, or taking part in a walk to raise funds for a worthy cause.

Try the following:

- Be empathetic and share your concern for others. You may not always know the exact words to say, but this is a good beginning.

- Be open to the perspectives of others and accept that others also want to have their views validated, even when they differ from yours.

- Be alert to internal dialogue that may show you're in a competitive mode rather than a compassionate mode.

- Say "Thank you." Find opportunities to express your gratitude through your words and actions.

- Help others.

- Smile. This is compassionate toward others and can put you in a positive frame of mind. If you can't readily think of what to smile about, do it anyway, or think about it for a moment until you can.

- Use humor, especially humor that acknowledges your shared humanity and reflects nonjudgment.

- Be mindful of when your compassion isn't welcome. Remember that not everyone feels equally comfortable with receiving compassion, in spite of your desire to cultivate self-compassion and compassion for others.

- Gain the courage to foster new habits of compassion, whether as a parent, supervisor, coworker, friend, neighbor, or fellow citizen.

- Be alert to threat systems—yours and those of the people you interact with.

- Compliment others.

EXERCISE

Identify an Act of Kindness

Martin Seligman recommends the following exercise as one that can powerfully enhance the way you show compassion to others.[8]

Identify one unexpected, kind thing that you can do for someone— and do it. It may even be a random act of kindness. When you do it, be mindful of what you experience throughout your body and the impact it has on your mood.

* * *

The practices in this chapter will help you and others achieve safety, connection, and reduced threat. And when you experience this, you'll flourish and be happier. Yes, we depend on others. And yes, there are numerous times to remember that everyone wants joy and contentment. Whether you try these practices with one person a day or several a week, remind yourself that each is an opportunity to be compassionate. By doing so, you acknowledge your shared humanity. And you'll help yourself and others become increasingly committed to the practice of healthy anger.

For Further Reflection

1. Identify a recent conflict with a friend or loved one in which you failed to communicate assertively. Review the assertiveness model in this chapter and identify how you might have assertively expressed yourself.

2. If you are partnered, what's your major challenge in committing to the terms of engagement outlined in this chapter? What can you do to overcome this challenge?

3. Recall a conflict at work. Identify an assertive response that addresses both your expectations and your conclusions.

4. Remind yourself that assertive communication may initially feel uncomfortable, especially if you haven't had much experience doing so. And others may need some time to get used to your new way of communicating as well.

5. During the next week, push your envelope to carry out acts of compassion. Savor the experience.

6. During the next week, look for examples of compassion between people and reflect on your thoughts and feelings when observing them.

7. Identify any challenges that might interfere with your behaving in a compassionate way to others.

CHAPTER 14

Committing to the Practice of Healthy Anger

This final chapter provides some guidelines to further your commitment to practice self-awareness, mindfulness, and self-compassion for healthy anger.

1. *Write down a list of reasons to practice healthy anger.* This will help you take ownership of your decision to live by the approaches described in this book. You'll see more clearly how these skills will benefit you. Your reasons should address:

   a. Why it's important

   b. What you hope to achieve

   c. How your life might be different

2. *Identify both short- and long-term goals.* Establish mini-goals that move you toward achieving larger goals. These might include, first, practicing mindfulness breathing and completing the Anger Log. Then gradually add other practices to your repertoire.

3. *Enter a time for practice in your daily calendar.* Pick a specific time each day to practice and to meditate. Add them to your daily calendar. That way, they'll become part of your daily routine rather than something you'll have to make time to do.

4. *Set up visual reminders.* Use sticky notes, photos, posters, pop-up reminders, or other formats to increase your mindfulness. Any reminder of the approaches in this book will strengthen your commitment to them.

5. *Be realistic in your expectations.* Expect baby steps in your progress. It takes time to absorb the material in this book and make it a natural part of your routine. Be realistic when determining how much time you plan to spend practicing each day.

6. *Complete an Anger Log frequently.* Healthy anger depends on your being mindful of and self-compassionate toward your internal experiences. Routinely completing the Anger Log offers a meaningful and powerful way to do this.

7. *Be mindful that all feelings and thoughts are temporary.* This is a key component of being mindful and is essential to developing healthy anger.

8. *Expect to experience anger in spite of progress.* Healthy anger means experiencing anger less often, less intensely, and for a shorter time. It requires being able to let tension go. Remember that your quickness to anger was developed to protect you from suffering.

9. *Savor moments of progress.* Be mindful about identifying and savoring the details of your progress. Be mindful about keeping track of the ways you've practiced healthy anger:

   a. Did you observe and alter your expectations?

   b. Were you more assertive in expressing your desires or needs?

   c. Were you able to consider other appraisals that helped reduce your quickness to anger?

   d. Were you successful in quickly becoming mindful of your body, feelings, self-talk, or images?

   e. Are you increasing your capacity to sit with your experience?

   Keep a journal. Every night, write down what you did that day to show your commitment to healthy anger. Be specific.

10. *Ask yourself how you can be self-compassionate.* Actively identify ways to be self-compassionate, rather than simply waiting for opportunities to do so. Keep these in mind and make self-compassion an integral part of your life.

11. *Ask yourself how you can be compassionate with others.* Actively identify ways to be compassionate with others, rather than simply waiting for opportunities to do so. Keep these in mind and make compassion for others an integral part of your life.

12. *Be especially mindful to be self-compassionate when you don't live up to your expectations.* The more judgmental you are when you relapse, the more likely it is you'll stop using these skills. Such judgment is devaluing and even shaming. You gain no benefit from hearing criticism when you haven't lived up to an expectation—whether it comes from yourself or others. Be mindful of self-talk that reflects tough love. Choose self-talk that shows compassion.

13. *Promise to persevere even when challenges arise.* We face many obstacles when learning new habits. Be mindful to expect them.

14. *Failure to practice once in a while doesn't alter progress.* Many studies show that failing to keep to a particular schedule once in a while has no lasting impact on learning. This is especially true if you can arouse self-compassion at such times.

15. *Be mindful of obstacles that inhibit your progress.* Be mindful of the identified challenges to anger, self-compassion, and compassion toward others. Evoke self-compassion and mindfulness to release the negative thoughts and discomfort that block you from progress.

16. *Seek support.* You may find it helpful to discuss your intentions and progress with someone. Ideally, seek support from others working on the same goals. Consider sharing with a friend, your partner, or a therapist.

17. *If you're in an intimate relationship, share your intentions and the content of the program with your partner.* Sharing the details of this program can help your partner be more sensitive to your needs, desires, and expectations. Your partner will understand when you voice your concern about stopping a discussion or need to take time to practice these skills. And certainly, it will help greatly if he or she reads this book.

18. *Identify factors that may impair your judgment.* Anything that interferes with your judgment may also affect your ability to fully use the approaches in this book. This may include alcohol or drug abuse or a mental disorder such as a mood disorder, attention difficulties, posttraumatic stress disorder, or a personality disorder. I strongly recommend that you receive treatment for these while working on or before beginning this program. If you're consulting

with a psychotherapist, let your counselor know you're using this program.

19. *Embrace self-discipline to gain freedom.* Committing to a long-term goal requires some sacrifice. Be mindful that your pleasure-seeking or discomfort-avoidant emotional brain may push you to focus on a short-term goal instead. But real freedom to more fully become who you want to be depends on self-discipline. Fulfilling any significant endeavor requires self-discipline. This holds true for overcoming destructive anger and embracing a new way of living.

Notes

CHAPTER 1. *Understanding Unhealthy Anger and Healthy Anger*

1. M. Reuter, B. Weber, B. Fiebach, et al., "The Biological Basis of Anger: Associations with Gene Coding for DARPP-32 (PP1R1B) and with the Amygdala Volume," *Behavioral Brain Research* 202 (2009): 179–183.

2. A. Johansson, P. Santtila, J. Corander, et al., "Genetic Effects on Anger Control and Their Interaction with Alcohol Intoxication: A Self-Report Study," *Biological Psychology* 85 (2010): 291–298.

3. X. Wang, R. Trivedi, F. Treiber, et al., "Genetic and Environmental Influences on Anger Expression, John Henryism, and Stressful Life Events: The Georgia Cardiovascular Twin Study," *Psychosomatic Medicine* 67, no. 1 (2005): 16–23.

4. M. Ghazinour and J. Richter, "Anger Related to Psychopathology, Temperament, and Character in Healthy Individuals: An Explorative Study," *Social Behavior and Personality* 37, no. 9 (2009): 1197–1212.

5. M. Rothbart and J. Bates, "Temperament," in *Handbook of Child Psychology, Vol. 3: Social, Emotional and Personality Development*, ed. William Damon, Ellen Eisenberg, and Richard Lerner (New York: Wiley, 1998), 105–176.

6. M. Reuter, "Population and Molecular Genetics of Anger and Aggression: Current State of the Art," in *International Handbook of Anger: Constituent and Concomitant Biological, Psychological, and Social Processes*, ed. M. Potegal, G. Stemmler, and C. Spielberger (New York: Springer Science, 2010), 27–37.

7. A. J. Bond and J. Wingrove, "The Neurochemistry and Psychopharmacology of Anger," in Potegal et al., *International Handbook of Anger*, 79–102.

8. M. D. Salter Ainsworth, "Attachments beyond Infancy," *American Psychologist* 44, no. 4 (1989): 709–716.

9. K. Lyons-Ruth and D. Jacobvitz, "Attachment Disorganization: Unresolved Loss, Relational Violence, and Lapses in Behavioral and Attentional Strategies," in *Handbook of Attachment: Theory, Research, and Clinical Applications*, ed. J. Cassidy and P. R. Shaver (New York: Guilford Press, 1999), 520–554.

10. M. D. Salter Ainsworth, M. C. Blehar, E. Waters, and S. D. Wall, *Patterns of Attachment* (Hillsdale, NJ: Erlbaum, 1978).

11. A. Schore, *Affect Dysregulation and Disorders of the Self* (New York: W. W. Norton, 2003).

12. K. Bartholomew and L. Horowitz, "Attachment Styles among Young Adults: A Test of a Four-Category Model," *Journal of Personality and Social Psychology* 61, no. 2 (1991): 226–244.

13. A. Troisi and A. D'Argenio, "The Relationship between Anger and Depression in a Clinical Sample of Young Men: The Role of Insecure Attachment," *Journal of Affective Disorders* 79, no. 1 (2004): 269–272.

14. W. Pollack, *Real Boys* (New York: Owl, 1999).

15. D. Siegel, *The Developing Mind* (New York: Guilford Press, 1999).

16. T. Denson, W. Pedersen, J. Ronquillo, and A. S. Nandy, "The Angry Brain: Neural Correlates of Anger, Angry Rumination, and Aggressive Personality," *Journal of Cognitive Neuroscience* 21, no. 4 (2009): 734.

17. Schore, *Affect Dysregulation and Disorders of the Self*, 80.

18. Siegel, *Developing Mind*, 24.

19. A. Pascual-Leone, C. Freitas, L. Oberman, et al., "Characterizing Brain Cortical Plasticity and Network Dynamics across the Age-Span in Health and Disease with TMS-EEG and TMS-fMRI," *Brain Topography* 24 (2011): 302–315.

20. P. Gilbert, *Compassion Focused Therapy* (New York: Routledge, 2010).

CHAPTER 2. *What Are the Challenges to Cultivating Healthy Anger?*

1. A. Storr, *Solitude* (New York: Free Press, 1988).

CHAPTER 3. *How Mindfulness and Mindfulness Meditation Can Help*

1. H. B. Aronson, *Buddhist Practice on Western Ground* (Boston: Shambhala, 2004).

2. C. L. M. Hill and J. A. Updegraff, "Mindfulness and Its Relationship to Emotional Regulation," *Emotion* 12, no. 1 (2012): 81–90.

3. J. Kabat-Zinn, *Coming to Our Senses: Healing Ourselves and the World through Mindfulness* (New York: Hyperion, 2005), 108.

4. D. Siegel, *Mindsight* (New York: Bantam, 2010), l.

5. M. Williams, J. Teasdale, Z. Segal, and J. Kabat-Zinn, *The Mindful Way through Depression: Freeing Yourself from Chronic Unhappiness* (New York: Guilford Press, 2007), 55.

6. B. Gunaratana, *Mindfulness in Plain English* (Somerville, MA: Wisdom, 2002), 33.

7. Ram Dass, *Journey of Awakening: A Meditator's Guidebook* (New York: Bantam, 1990), 45.

8. Williams et al., *Mindful Way through Depression*.

9. M. Williams and D. Penman, *Mindfulness: An Eight-Week Plan for Finding Peace in a Frantic World* (New York: Rodale, 2011), 84.

10. Thich Nhat Hanh, *The Miracle of Mindfulness* (Boston: Beacon, 1987), 20.

11. His Holiness the Dalai Lama, *Beyond Religion: Ethics for a Whole World* (New York: Houghton Mifflin Harcourt, 2011), 165.

12. Gunaratana, *Mindfulness in Plain English*, 33.

13. D. Simons, "The Monkey Business Illusion," at www.youtube.com/watch?v=0 -HR9WfdYSY.

CHAPTER 4. *The Role of Self-Compassion*

1. Gilbert, *Compassion Focused Therapy*.

2. P. Gilbert, "Evolved Minds and Compassion in the Therapeutic Relationship," in *The Therapeutic Relationship in the Cognitive Behavioral Psychotherapies*, ed. P. Gilbert and R. Leahy (London: Routledge, 2007), 106–142.

3. C. Germer, *The Mindful Path to Self-Compassion* (New York: Guilford Press, 2009), 33.
4. Ibid.
5. K. Neff, *Self-Compassion* (New York: HarperCollins, 2011).
6. K. Neff, "Self-Compassion: An Alternative Conceptualization of a Healthier Attitude toward Oneself," *Self and Identity* 2 (2003): 85–102.
7. C. Peterson and M. Seligman, *Character Strengths and Virtues* (New York: Oxford University Press, 2004), 106.
8. J. Khandro Rinpoche, "Lion's Roar: Buddhist Wisdom for Our Time," at www.lionsroar.com/?s=compassion+and+wisdom.
9. D. V. Jeste and J. C. Harris, "Wisdom: A Neuroscience Perspective," *JAMA* 14 (2010): 1602–1603.
10. Neff, *Self-Compassion*, 80.
11. Ibid., 83.

CHAPTER 5. *Cultivating Self-Compassion*

1. D. Siegel, *The Mindful Brain: Reflections and Attunement in the Cultivation of Well-Being* (New York: W. W. Norton, 2007).
2. Gilbert, *Compassion Focused Therapy*.
3. C. Carter, "Neuroendocrine Perspectives on Social Attachment and Love," *Psychoneuroendocrinology* 23 (1998): 779–818.
4. K. Grewen, S. Girdler, J. Amico, and K. C. Light, "Effects of Partner Support on Resting Oxytocin, Cortisol, Norepinephrine, and Blood Pressure before and after Warm Partner Contact," *Psychosomatic Medicine* 67, no. 4 (2005): 531–538.
5. M. Kosfeld, M. Heinrichs, P. J. Zak, et al., "Oxytocin Increases Trust in Humans," *Nature* 435 (2005): 673–676.
6. O. Longe, F. Maratos, P. Gilbert, et al., "Having a Word with Yourself: Neural Correlates of Self-Criticism and Self-Reassurance," *NeuroImage* 49 (2010): 1849–1856.
7. D. Keltner, "Secrets of the Vagus Nerve," at www.greatergood.berkeley.edu/gg_live/science_meaningful_life_videos/speakers/dacher_keltner/secrets_of_the_vagus_nerve.
8. S. W. Porges, *The Polyvagal Theory* (New York: W. W. Norton, 2011), 16.
9. J. Smith, *Relaxation, Meditation, and Mindfulness* (New York: Springer, 2005).
10. Gilbert, *Compassion Focused Therapy*, 160.
11. S. Carson, *Your Creative Brain* (New York: Jossey-Bass, 2012).

CHAPTER 6. *Mindfulness and Self-Compassion for Your Body*

1. A. Miller, *The Body Never Lies: The Lingering Effects of Cruel Parenting* (New York: W. W. Norton, 2005), 207.
2. Williams et al., *Mindful Way through Depression*.

3. Germer, *Mindful Path to Self-Compassion*, 49.

4. H. Benson, *The Relaxation Response* (New York: Avon, 1976).

5. S. Khalfa, S. Dalla Bella, M. Roy, et al., "Effects of Relaxing Music on Salivary Cortisol Level after Psychological Stress," *Annals of the New York Academy of Sciences* 999 (2003): 374–376.

6. E. Labbe, N. Schmidt, J. Babin, and M. Pharr, "Coping with Stress: The Effectiveness of Different Types of Music," *Applied Psychophysiology and Biofeedback* 32, no. 3/4 (2007): 163–168.

CHAPTER 7. *A Framework for Understanding Anger*

1. Aronson, *Buddhist Practice on Western Ground*, 113.

2. His Holiness the Dalai Lama and Paul Ekman, *Emotional Awareness* (New York: Henry Holt, 2008), 23.

3. B. Golden, *Healthy Anger: How to Help Children and Teens Manage Their Anger* (New York: Oxford University Press, 2003).

4. R. Pond, T. Kashdan, N. Dewall, et al., "Emotional Differentiation Moderates Aggressive Tendencies in Angry People: A Daily Diary Analysis," *Emotion* 12, no. 2 (2012): 326–337.

5. D. Goleman, *Emotional Intelligence* (New York: Bantam, 1997), 43.

6. H. H. the Dalai Lama and Ekman, *Emotional Awareness*, 75.

7. K. Mizuno, *Essentials of Buddhism* (Tokyo: Kosei, 1996), 154.

8. D. Burns, *Feeling Good* (New York: Avon, 1980).

CHAPTER 9. *Mindfulness and Self-Compassion for Your Feelings*

1. D. Nelis, I. Kosou, J. Quoidbach, et al., "Increasing Emotional Competence Improves Psychological and Physical Well-Being, Social Relationships, and Employability," *Emotion* 11, no. 2 (2011): 354–356.

2. Goleman, *Emotional Intelligence*, 47.

3. A. Fogel, *The Psychophysiology of Self-Awareness* (New York: W. W. Norton, 2009), 47.

4. Germer, *Mindful Path to Self-Compassion*, 66.

5. S. Hayes and K. Strosahl, *A Practical Guide to Acceptance and Commitment Therapy* (New York: Springer Science + Business Media, 2004), 27.

6. A. Freud, *The Ego and the Mechanisms of Defense* (New York: International Universities Press, 1946).

7. L. Abrams, "Anger and Anxiety: Two Sides of the Same Coin?" *gradPSYCH*, March 2013, at www.apa.org/gradpsych/2013/03/research.aspx.

8. R. Simon and K. Lively, "Sex, Anger and Depression," *Social Forces* 88, no. 4 (2010): 1543–1568.

9. F. Busch, M. Rudden, and T. Shapiro, *Psychodynamic Treatment of Depression* (Arlington VA: American Psychiatric Press, 2004).

10. J. Bradshaw, *Healing the Shame That Binds You*, 2nd ed. (Deerfield Beach, FL: Health Communications, 2005), 10.

11. J. P. Tangney and K. W. Fischer, *The Self-Conscious Emotions—The Psychology of Guilt, Embarrassment, and Pride* (London: Guilford Press, 1995).

12. P. Gilbert, *The Compassionate Mind: A New Approach to Life's Challenges* (Oakland, CA: New Harbinger, 2009), 315.

13. M. Lewis, *Shame: The Exposed Self* (New York: Free Press, 1995).

14. H. Lewis, *Shame and Guilt in Neurosis* (New York: International Universities Press, 1971).

15. P. Gilbert and S. Proctor, "Compassionate Mind Training for People with High Shame and Self-Criticism: An Overview and Pilot Study of a Group Therapy Approach," *Clinical Psychology and Psychotherapy* 13 (2006): 353–379.

CHAPTER 10. *Mindfulness and Self-Compassion for Your Thoughts*

1. Burns, *Feeling Good.*

2. H. Kushner, *How Good Do We Have to Be?* (Boston: Little, Brown, 1997), 9.

CHAPTER 11. *Self-Compassion for Healthy Anger*

1. S. Salzberg, *Loving-Kindness: The Revolutionary Art of Happiness* (Boston: Shambhala, 2002), 39.

2. Germer, *Mindful Path to Self-Compassion*, 134.

3. A. H. Harris, F. M. Luskin, S. V. Benisovich, et al., "Effects of a Group Forgiveness Intervention on Forgiveness, Perceived Stress and Trait Anger: A Randomized Trial," *Journal of Clinical Psychology* 62, no. 6 (2006): 715–733.

4. J. Friedberg, S. Suchday, and D. Shelov, "The Impact of Forgiveness on Cardiovascular Reactivity and Recovery," *International Journal of Psychophysiology* 65, no. 2 (2007): 87–94.

5. J. W. Carson, F. J. Keefe, V. Goli, et al., "Forgiveness and Chronic Low Back Pain: A Preliminary Study Examining the Relationship of Forgiveness to Pain, Anger and Physiological Distress," *Journal of Pain* 6 (2005): 84–91.

6. M. A. Waltman, D. C. Russel, C. T. Coyle, et al., "The Effects of a Forgiveness Intervention on Patients with Coronary Artery Disease, *Psychology and Health* 24, no. 1 (2009): 11–27.

7. S. Braithwaite, E. Selby, and F. D. Fincham, "Forgiveness and Relationship Satisfaction: Mediating Mechanisms," *Journal of Family Psychology* 25 (2011): 551–559.

8. R. Casarjian, *Forgiveness: A Bold Choice for a Peaceful Heart* (New York: Bantam, 1992), 84.

CHAPTER 12. *Mindfulness, Self-Compassion, and Compassion for Others*

1. P. Gilbert, "Introducing Compassion-Focused Therapy," *Advances in Psychiatric Treatment* 15 (2009): 199–208.

2. Germer, *Mindful Path to Self-Compassion*, 161.

3. J. Hopkins, *Cultivating Compassion* (New York: Broadway, 2001), 95.

4. L. Ladner, *The Lost Art of Compassion: Discovering the Practice of Happiness in the Meeting of Buddhism and Psychology* (New York: HarperOne, 2004), 153.

CHAPTER 13. *Self-Compassionate and Compassionate Interactions with Others*

1. R. Alberti and M. Emmons, *Your Perfect Right: Assertiveness and Equality in Your Life and Relationships*, 9th ed. (Atascadero, CA: Impact, 2008).
2. A. Gordon and S. Chen, "The Role of Sleep in Interpersonal Conflict," at http://spp.sagepub.com/content/early/2013/05/13/1948550613488952.abstract.
3. B. L. Frederickson, *Love 2.0: Creating Happiness and Health in Moments of Connection* (New York: Penguin, 2013), 17.
4. J. Gottman and N. Silver, *The Seven Principles for Making Marriage Work* (New York: Crown, 1999).
5. D. Goleman, *Social Intelligence* (New York: Bantam, 2006).
6. P. Bronson, *Why Do I Love These People?* (New York: Random House, 2005).
7. T. Goodrich, Baylor Media Communications, "What Warring Couples Want: Power, Not Apologies, Baylor Study Shows," July 8, 2013, at www.baylor.edu/mediacommunications/news.php?action=story&story=131229.
8. M. Seligman, *Flourish* (New York: Atria, 2013), 21.

Resources

Websites

The following websites offer information and many types of mindfulness and self-compassion exercises. You may want to try several of the exercises to determine which ones fit you best.

Anger

American Psychological Association
www.apa.org/topics/anger/control.aspx

Anger Management Techniques
www.anger-management-techniques.org/index.htm

Helpguide.org
www.helpguide.org/mental/anger_management_control_tips_techniques.htm

Mindfulness Meditation

Headspace
www.headspace.com
This application, available through iTunes, provides guided meditations and addresses a variety of issues such as anxiety, creativity, and relationships.

iTunes
www.apple.com/itunes
iTunes offers a wide variety of mindfulness meditation MP3s, including some by Jon Kabat-Zinn, Mark Williams, and Daniel Goleman.

University of Massachusetts Medical School, Center for Mindfulness in Medicine, Health Care, and Society
www.umassmed.edu/cfm/index.aspx
Courses with Jon Kabat-Zinn, PhD.

Self-Compassion

The Campaign for Love and Forgiveness
http://loveandforgive.org/loveandforgive/home
Information about the Campaign for Forgiveness Project.

Center for Mindful Self-Compassion
http://centerformsc.org
This site offers resources and helps promote self-compassion.

Charter for Compassion
http://charterforcompassion.org
This site offers a petition and a charter that help promote compassion.

Fetzer Institute
http://fetzer.org
Resources on love, forgiveness, and compassion in American society.

The Greater Good Science Center
http://greatergood.berkeley.edu
This site focuses on the science of a meaningful life. It offers articles, workshops, and resources on themes of gratitude, altruism, compassion, empathy, forgiveness, happiness, and mindfulness.

Mindful Self-Compassion
http://mindfulselfcompassion.org
Directed by Christopher Germer, this site offers exercises, publications, and resources on mindfulness and self-compassion.

Rick Hanson, PhD: Resources for Happiness, Love, and Wisdom
www.rickhanson.net/event/natural-contentment
Rick Hanson offers meditations on self-compassion and contentment.

Scoop It
www.scoop.it/t/teaching-empathy
This site provides articles about how to be more empathetic and compassionate.

Self-Compassion
http://selfcompassion.org
Kristin Neff's website offers insight, exercises, and resources on self-compassion.

The Self-Compassionate Project
http://theselfcompassionproject.com
This site offers resources to help foster self-compassion.

Suggested Readings

Beck, Aaron T. *Prisoners of Hate: The Cognitive Basis of Anger, Hostility and Violence.* New York: HarperCollins, 1999.

Brach, Tara. *Radical Acceptance: Embracing Your Life with the Heart of a Buddha.* New York: Bantam, 2003.

Davidson, Richard J., with Sharon Begley. *The Emotional Life of Your Brain.* New York: Plume, 2013.

Enright, Robert D. *The Forgiving Life.* Washington, DC: American Psychological Association, 2012.

Epstein, Mark. *Going on Being: Buddhism and the Way of Change.* New York: Basic Books, 2001.

Hanson, Rick. *Just One Thing: Developing a Buddha Brain One Simple Practice at a Time*. Oakland, CA: New Harbinger, 2011.

Hanson, Rick, and Richard Mendius. *Buddha's Brain: The Practical Neuroscience of Happiness, Love and Wisdom*. Oakland, CA: New Harbinger, 2009.

Harbin, Thomas. *Beyond Anger: A Guide for Men: How to Free Yourself from the Grip of Anger and Get More out of Life*. Cambridge, MA: DaCapo Press, 2000.

Kabat-Zinn, Jon. *Coming to Our Senses: Healing Ourselves and the World through Mindfulness Meditation*. New York: Piatkus, 2005.

———. *Mindfulness for Beginners*. Boulder, CO: Sounds True, 2006.

———. *Wherever You Go There You Are: Mindfulness Meditation in Everyday Life*. New York: Hyperion, 1994.

Kundtz, David. *Quiet Mind: One Minute Retreats from a Busy World*. San Francisco: Canari Press, 2000.

Lerner, Harriet. *The Dance of Anger*. New York: Perennial Currents, 2005.

Lyubomirsky, Sonja. *The How of Happiness*. New York: Penguin, 2007.

Mackenzie, Mary. *Peaceful Living*. Encinitas, CA: PuddleDancer, 2005.

McKay, Matthew, and Peter Rogers. *The Anger Control Workbook*. Oakland, CA: New Harbinger, 2000.

Robinson, Joe. *Don't Miss Your Life*. Hoboken, NJ: John Wiley, 2011.

Rubin, Theodore. *Compassion and Self-Hate*. New York: Touchstone, 1975.

Seligman, Martin E. P. *Authentic Happiness*. New York: Free Press, 2002.

———. *Flourish*. New York: Atria (Simon and Schuster), 2011.

———. *Learned Optimism: How to Change Your Mind and Life*. New York: Vintage, 2011 (reprint).

Shapiro, Ed, and Deb Shapiro. *Be the Change: How Meditation Can Transform You and the World*. New York: Sterling, 2009.

Tafrate, Raymond C., and Howard Kassinove. *Anger Management for Everyone*. Atascadero, CA: Impact, 2009.

Teasedale, John, Mark Williams, and Zindel Segal. *The Mindful Way Workbook: An 8-Week Program to Free Yourself from Depression and Emotional Distress*. New York: Guilford Press, 2014.

Thich Nhat Hanh. *Anger: Wisdom for Cooling the Flames*. New York: Riverhead Trade, 2002.

Movies

Several movies powerfully explore complex characters who have learned to deal with anger.

American History X (1998)

In a Better World (2010)

Reservation Road (2007)

Twelve Angry Men (1957)

Index